MEDICAL RESEARCH + TECHNOLOGY

◤ by Alexandra Morris

Content Consultant

James Donelson, PhD
Associate Professor of Chemistry
Missouri Southern State University

Essential Library

An Imprint of Abdo Publishing | abdopublishing.com

CUTTING EDGE
SCIENCE +
TECHNOLOGY

abdopublishing.com

Published by Abdo Publishing, a division of ABDO, PO Box 398166, Minneapolis, Minnesota 55439. Copyright © 2016 by Abdo Consulting Group, Inc. International copyrights reserved in all countries. No part of this book may be reproduced in any form without written permission from the publisher. Essential Library™ is a trademark and logo of Abdo Publishing.

Printed in the United States of America, North Mankato, Minnesota
092015
012016

THIS BOOK CONTAINS
RECYCLED MATERIALS

Cover Photo: iStockphoto/Thinkstock
Interior Photos: Ulrich Baumgarten/Getty Images, 4–5; iStockphoto, 7, 38–39, 41, 45, 48–49, 62, 78, 98; Lynn Hey/AP Images, 9; Rex Features/AP Images, 11, 55; Andrew Milligan/Press Association/AP Images, 12; Matt Dunham/AP Images, 15; Katarzyna Bialasiewicz/iStockphoto, 16–17; Trisha Leeper/WireImage/Getty Images, 19; Red Line Editorial, 21, 23, 35; Philippe Plailly/Science Source, 25; Jessica Wilson/Science Source, 26; BONY/SIPA/AP Images, 28–29; Sci-Somm Studios/Science Source, 31; Martin McCarthy/iStockphoto, 37; Rick Friedman/Corbis, 47; Shutterstock Images, 51; GARO/Phanie Sarl/Corbis, 53; Pallava Bagla/Corbis, 58–59; Mary Martin/Science Source, 65; Anya Ivanova/Shutterstock Images, 66; Abbas Dulleh/AP Images, 69; Koichi Mitsui/AFLO/Nippon News/Corbis, 70–71; Simon Isabelle/SIPA/AP Images, 73; Solent News/Rex Features/AP Images, 74; Mücahiddin Şentürk/iStockphoto, 76; J. Pat Carter/AP Images, 80–81; Patrick Farrell/Miami Herald/MCT/Newscom, 83; Karen Kasmauski/SuperStock, 85; Morry Gash/AP Images, 86; Rich Pedroncelli/AP Images, 89; Karen Kasmauski/Corbis, 90–91; Friso Gentsch/Picture-Alliance/DPA/AP Images, 93; Dieter Nagl/AFP/Getty Images, 95; Dave Zajac/Record-Journal/AP Images, 96

Editor: Melissa York
Series Designer: Craig Hinton

Library of Congress Control Number: 2015945633

Cataloging-in-Publication Data
Morris, Alexandra.
Medical research and technology / Alexandra Morris.
  p. cm. -- (Cutting-edge science and technology)
ISBN 978-1-62403-916-4 (lib. bdg.)
Includes bibliographical references and index.
1. Medical technology--Juvenile literature. 2. Medical innovations--Juvenile literature.   I. Title.
610.28--dc23

2015945633

CONTENTS

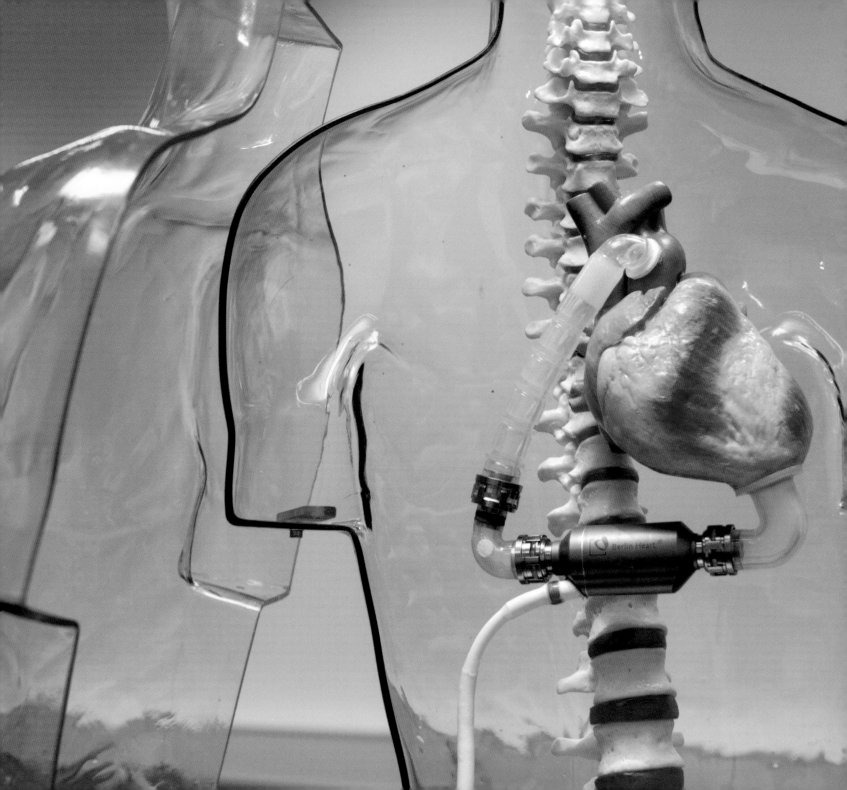

GROWING NEW
ORGANS

More than 120,000 people in the United States are waiting for a lifesaving organ transplant at any given time. Yet in 2014, less than one-quarter of these patients received transplants. The gap between the number of patients who need an organ and the number of organs available to be transplanted continues to widen. Meanwhile, the costs are fatal. Each day, 22 people die while waiting for a transplant.[1] Organ shortages have increasingly become a public health crisis.

Even in cases in which a patient receives a transplant from a donor, there is a still a strong chance their body will reject the organ. To combat this, many patients need to take drugs that suppress their immune system so it doesn't attack the organ for the rest of their lives. Although these drugs, known as immunosuppressants, are vital for organ recipients, they weaken the immune system, which leaves the body less resistant to infectious diseases and cancer.

Until doctors are able to grow more types of organs in the lab, artificial means such as heart pumps help some patients.

Growing Organs in the Lab

But what if there were a way to engineer an organ using a patient's own cells? This would eliminate the need for an organ donor and also help ensure the organ wouldn't be rejected. Immunosuppressant drugs would be less necessary. After all, the body isn't likely to reject the patient's own cells.

Kidneys filter waste from the blood, creating urine the bladder holds until it is released.

It may sound like science fiction, but there are patients today who are living healthy lives with bladders, urethras, and vaginas that were grown inside a laboratory. In 2001, a research team from Wake Forest University, led by Dr. Anthony Atala, became the first group to successfully transplant lab-grown human bladders into patients using the patients' own cells. Seven children from ages four to 19 who had poor bladder function received the transplants.

To create the bladders, scientists took a small piece of the diseased bladder tissue (roughly half the size of a postage stamp), gently took apart the cells, and grew the cells outside the body. They then created a biodegradable scaffold, or frame, made of polyglycolic acid and collagen. Polyglycolic acid is a man-made material used to make some plastics and skin-care products. Collagen is a protein found in connective

The First Organ Transplant

The first successful human organ transplant was performed in 1954. The patient, 23-year-old Richard Herrick, had been experiencing kidney failure. To save his brother, Herrick's identical twin, Ronald, agreed to donate one of his own kidneys. More than 30 years later, the surgeon who performed the transplant, Dr. Joseph Murray, received the prestigious Nobel Prize in Physiology or Medicine for his work. In order to expand the pool of donors beyond identical twins, however, researchers needed to find ways to prevent organ rejection. Eventually they made another breakthrough: the successful development of treatments to suppress the immune system, which enabled the body to accept the new organ.

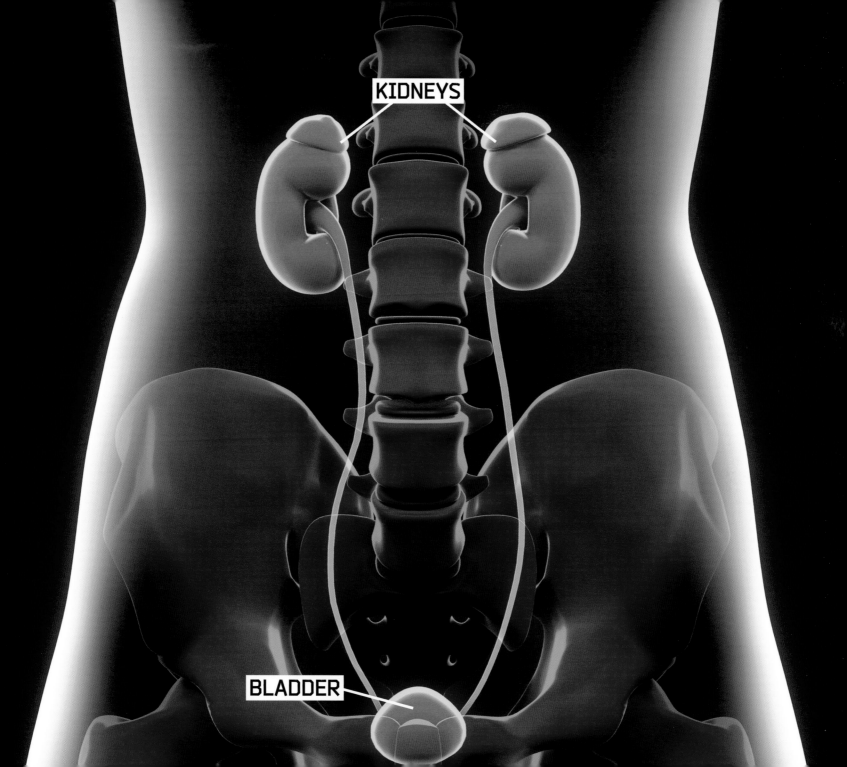

A Bladder Matter

Luke Massella was born with spina bifida, a birth defect that paralyzed his bladder. By the time he was ten, Luke had been through 16 surgeries. His poor bladder function eventually caused urine to back up in his kidneys, which prevented them from functioning correctly. He experienced kidney failure and faced a lifetime of dialysis. Dialysis is a life-support treatment that performs the role of the kidneys. The patient is hooked up to a machine that filters out waste and excess water from the blood. But it is time-consuming, requiring three four-hour treatments each week. It was then that Luke and his parents decided to try an experimental surgery, a lab-grown bladder transplant. Luke was one of the first patients to receive a bladder generated from his own cells. Ten years later, in 2011, Luke was invited onstage to join Dr. Anthony Atala of the Wake Forest Institute of Regenerative Medicine, whose team had developed the bladder, during a presentation. Luke, who by then was a sophomore at the University of Connecticut, was asked about his experience as a recipient of an engineered bladder. "This surgery came along and basically made me who I am today and saved my life," he said.[2]

tissue, such as skin. The researchers shaped the scaffold to resemble the bladder, then placed a layer of the patient's muscle cells on the outside. A layer of the patient's laboratory-grown bladder-lining cells were placed on the inside. Finally, the researchers put the structure and cells in a bioreactor, a device that can grow cells and tissues under controlled conditions. The cells could then grow and multiply to create the functional organ. The process took approximately two months. The organs were then transplanted into the patients.

Five years later, Atala and his team announced the seven patients who had received the lab-grown bladders showed no signs of complications. The transplants had been a success.

Atala's research continues. In a study published in 2014, he reported that his team had successfully implanted vaginas in four teenage girls who were born with a rare genetic condition that prevented their vaginas from fully developing. Again, the team used the patients' own cells to develop the organs.

Anthony **Atala**
(1958–)

Peruvian-born Dr. Anthony Atala is a researcher, surgeon, and director of the Wake Forest Institute for Regenerative Medicine. He is a pioneer in the field of tissue engineering. His research has been featured among the top medical breakthroughs by *Time* magazine, *Discover* magazine, and a number of other publications. He has received prestigious awards honoring his contribution to medicine and technology. His team of researchers is currently working on a number of projects related to tissue and organ replacement, including the three-dimensional printing of a human kidney. The team has designed a printer that can print kidney cells, as well as the biomaterials needed to hold these cells together. Atala hopes three-dimensional printing will someday help address the global organ shortage.

Then the researchers followed the patients for eight years. At the end of this period, they found that the young women had healthy vaginas with no abnormalities.

New findings continue to emerge in the field of organ development. From surgeons in Sweden who developed the first synthetic windpipe transplanted in a cancer patient to future plans to transplant lab-grown penises in patients who have penile cancer, traumatic injury, or were born with abnormalities, there is seemingly no end to the possibilities in the field.

Creating organs such as skin, windpipes, bladders, and vaginas were huge successes in the field, but the biggest research challenges lie ahead. The complexities of these flat or saclike organs pale in comparison to solid organs such as kidneys, lungs, the heart, and the liver. Creating the intricate network of blood vessels necessary to keep these organs alive has proven an enormous challenge for scientists.

Doctors created a scaffold from a new type of plastic and added the patient's cells to create the first synthetic windpipe.

Three-Dimensional Printing

Many scientists believe the real future of organ generation lies in three-dimensional printing. Three-dimensional objects begin as a digital file. Successive layers of material (in this case, human cells) are printed, or laid down. This "bio-ink" is layered onto a base material such as a gel or a sugar. Once the organ has been printed, it is placed in a bioreactor before being transplanted into a patient.

Three-dimensional printing has produced bones, ears, windpipes, a jawbone, and blood vessels. But researchers around the world are setting their sights even higher: bioprinting a solid organ. First on their wish list? A kidney.

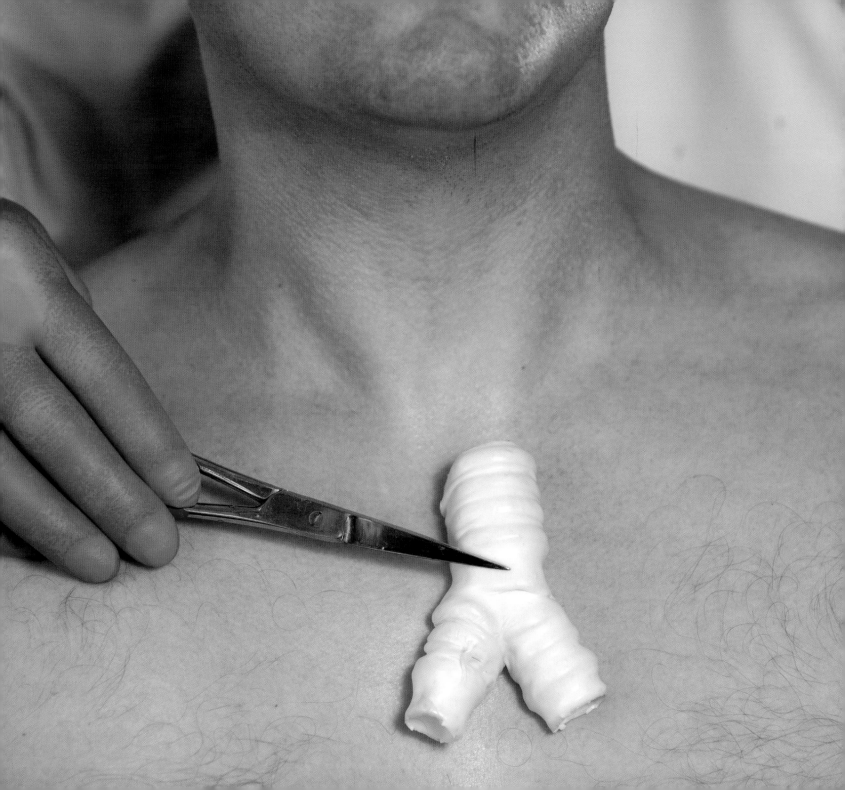

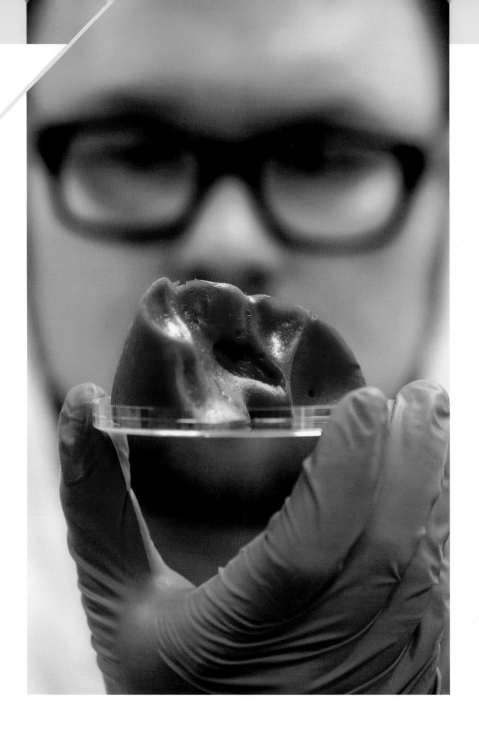

This nonfunctioning liver was created using a three-dimensional printer.

Kidneys are one of the most challenging organs to develop, but they have the greatest potential for saving lives. More than 80 percent of patients on the US organ transplant waiting list need a kidney. That's more than 100,000 people. Yet in 2014, only approximately 17,000 kidney transplants took place in the United States.[3] Developing the field of three-dimensional printing and bioengineering organs to fill this gap is crucial. Replacing donor organs with lab-grown ones has the potential to revolutionize the practice of medicine.

Challenges for 3-D Printing

The biggest challenge for printing a kidney is creating the intricate network of blood vessels, including veins, arteries, and tiny capillaries. The network carries nutrients throughout the kidney and filters out waste. Without this network of channels, the kidney will not function.

Capillaries can be as small as a few microns wide. A micron is one-millionth of a meter. For reference, a human hair is approximately 100 microns in diameter. Even the highest resolution printers are currently unable to create structures that won't collapse in on themselves. It's particularly difficult given that these tiny structures are often printed onto a soft gel, which doesn't offer much support.

However, in the summer of 2014, researchers from Harvard and the University of Sydney announced they had successfully created a network of functional capillaries using three-dimensional printing technology. The researchers developed tiny fibers that served as the mold for the network of blood vessels. The structure was then covered with a protein-based material that became solid when a light was shone on it. When the fibers were removed, a network of tiny channels coated with cells remained. Within a week, capillaries were formed. This latest finding is likely to have huge implications for organ development.

Living Ink

In 2000, medical researcher Dr. Thomas Boland began tinkering with the printer in his lab at Clemson University. At the time, printers had been successfully printing genes, but none had printed other biomaterials. Boland and his team reconfigured a regular desktop printer to print with *E. coli* bacteria, then moved on to larger mammalian cells. Printing with bio-ink involves depositing drops of living cells or other biomaterials onto a base material such as a gel or sugar. Multiple ink cartridges can be used to deposit different cell types, such as organ-specific cells or blood vessel cells. After the organ has been bioprinted, it is put into a bioreactor to finish growing before it is transplanted.

The Cutting Edge of Medicine

Human life expectancy has doubled over the past 150 years.[4] As humanity ages, we face new and unforeseen medical challenges. But technology has transformed the practice of medicine, helping doctors deliver cheaper, faster, and more efficient care to patients. Cutting-edge advances in research and technology allow for patient care that once seemed impossible.

A researcher demonstrates placing stem cells onto a synthetic plastic ear. The research facility is also working on developing transplantable noses.

Engineering organs for transplant is just one example of the enormous power of modern medicine. From medical robots that monitor patients' vital signs to self-tracking devices that allow patients to provide physicians with daily updates on chronic conditions to the development of therapies specifically targeted to a person's genetic makeup, recent advances in health care have revolutionized the practice of medicine.

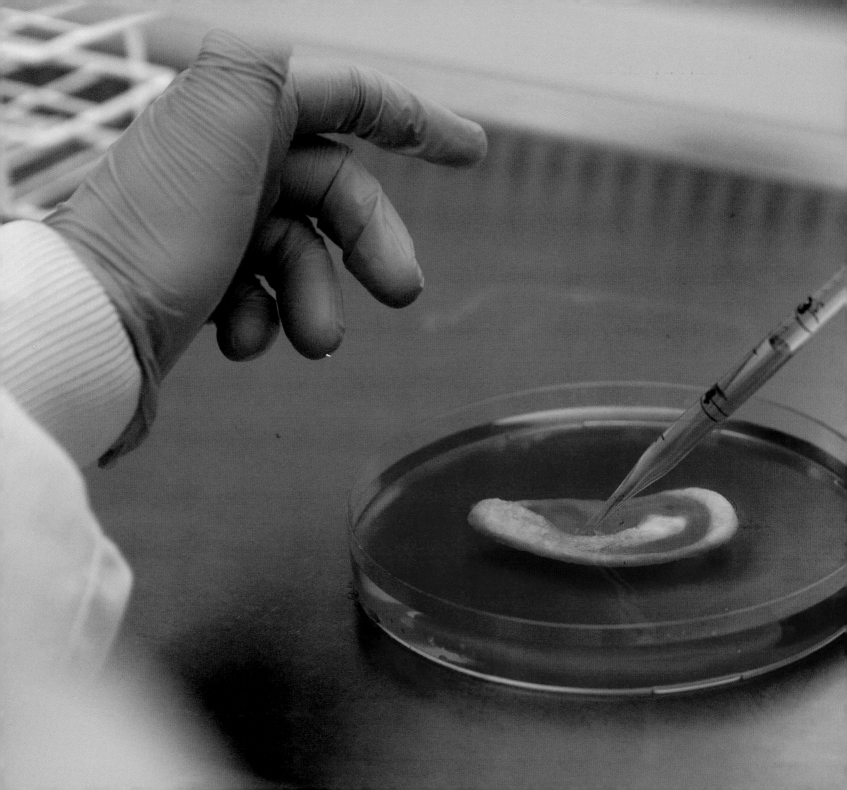

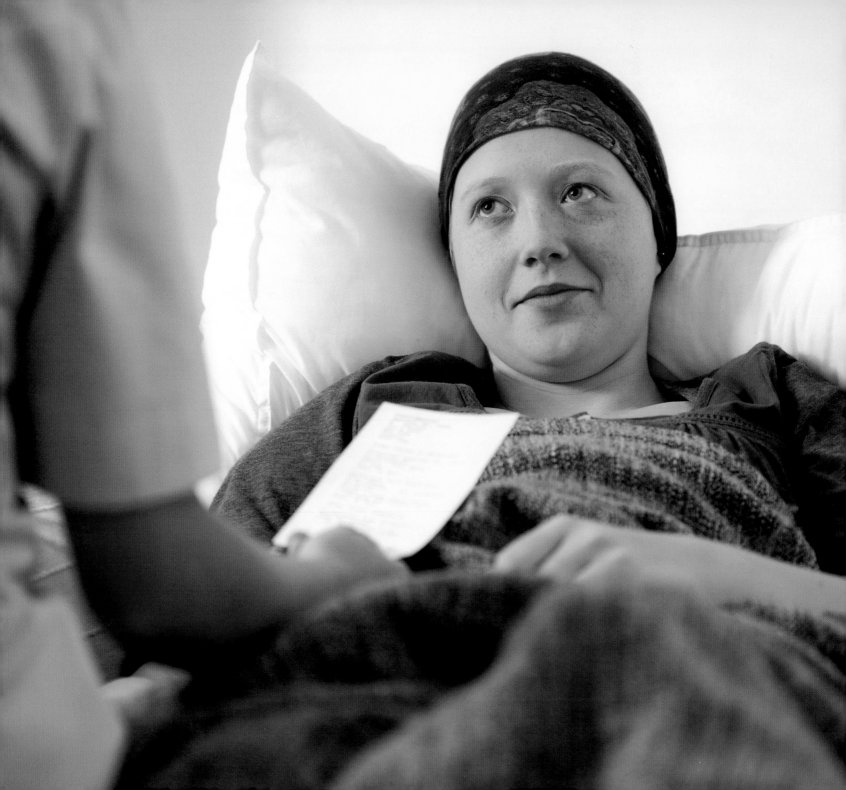

TWO

FIGHTING CANCER
WITH THE
IMMUNE SYSTEM

Cancer is a large family of diseases that involve abnormal cell growth. Cells grow out of control, forming lumps or masses called tumors. Surgery, radiation, and chemotherapy have been the primary defenses against cancer for years. These treatments work to attack tumors directly and kill the cancer cells. Radiation therapy uses invisible, high-energy waves to kill cancer cells. Chemotherapy uses drugs or other chemicals. Today, there is growing interest in a form of treatment known as immunotherapy. This therapy activates the immune system, the body's natural defense system, to fight the disease. The challenge has been to develop a treatment that can stimulate the immune system in the right way so it fights off infection without turning against normal tissue.

Chemotherapy can cause hair loss and make patients feel nauseous.

The Beginnings of Immunotherapy

In the 1890s, a cancer patient who had a rare sarcoma (a type of cancer that develops from certain tissues, such as bone or muscle) growing in his neck caught the attention of New York surgeon William Coley. Although the patient had had multiple operations to remove the tumor, the cancer had come back each time. Finally his doctors declared his cancer incurable. The patient then became infected with streptococcal bacteria, which can cause illnesses ranging from strep throat to pneumonia. Since there were no antibiotics at the time, his immune system kicked in to fight off the infection on its own. As the infection cleared, the cancer mysteriously cleared along with it. Coley tried to replicate this event by injecting streptococcal cultures in other cancer patients. In some cases, the method was successful and the tumors shrank. His initial research was published in 1893, the first report to describe a serious attempt at what would someday be known as cancer immunotherapy. Although Coley achieved some success over the next 40 years, his research was largely ignored. It was difficult to reproduce and it was not considered scientifically rigorous.

Breakthrough of the Year

In December 2013, *Science* magazine named cancer immunotherapy the scientific "breakthrough of the year."[1] *Science* Editor-in-Chief Marcia McNutt, whose own father died of lung cancer, wrote in an editorial: "Breakthroughs in cancer immunotherapy may have arrived too late for my father, but there are many cancer patients around the world whose lives could potentially be extended as we learn more about this promising new approach."[2] In fact, the concept of cancer immunotherapy had been around for more than 100 years, but it wasn't considered a breakthrough treatment until recent years.

Dr. James Allison of the University of Texas MD Anderson Cancer Center is largely credited with putting immunotherapy in the spotlight. Allison's research has helped scientists understand how the immune system is activated and how it is stopped when confronted with cancer. His discoveries have enabled the development of an entirely different drug to treat cancer.

Allison, center, won a Breakthrough Prize, given for the year's best scientific work, in 2013.

Allison was just 11 years old when his mother died from lymphoma in 1960. He recalled watching her suffer from the side effects of radiation treatment. He lost several other family members to cancer, and he was diagnosed with prostate cancer himself in 2005. Fortunately, the cancer was caught early and successfully treated by removing the organ. Allison has spent his career exploring the immune system. He had a particular interest in a type of immune cell that fights off infection, known as the T-cell.

T-Cells

In 1987, a group of French researchers discovered a new protein on the surface of a T-cell. It was initially thought this protein, called cytotoxic T-lymphocyte antigen 4 (CTLA-4), was responsible for speeding up the immune system so it could attack infections. But Allison and his colleagues determined it had the opposite effect—it inhibited the activity of immune cells. This mechanism holds the immune system in check, preventing it from attacking healthy tissue. But because the protein was blocking T-cells from activating, it was also preventing the immune system from attacking cancer. Researchers discovered that it is possible to temporarily block CTLA-4 long enough to allow immune cells to mount a response to an infection, but not so long that it would cause a fatal response. Allison's mission? Free the T-cells from CTLA-4.

In the mid-1990s, Allison and his team tested an antibody that blocked CTLA-4 in mice with cancerous tumors. The team found the tumors stopped growing in the mice that received the antibody, and the cancer began to disappear. The tumors continued growing in the mice that did not receive the antibody. After six weeks, nine of the ten treated mice were fine, but all of the untreated mice had died.

How T-Cells Work

In the human body's immune response, a type of cell called a phagocyte "eats" bacteria. Parts of the bacteria, now called antigens, rise to the surface of the phagocyte. The helper T-cell discovers the antigens and is activated.

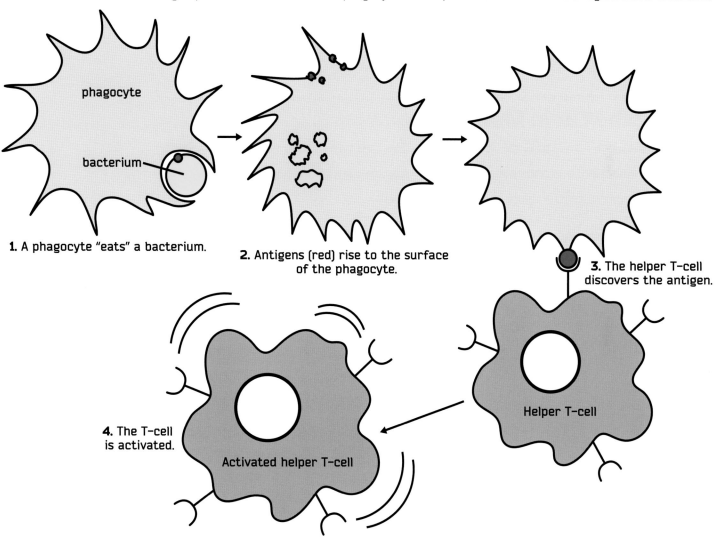

1. A phagocyte "eats" a bacterium.

2. Antigens (red) rise to the surface of the phagocyte.

3. The helper T-cell discovers the antigen.

4. The T-cell is activated.

Activated helper T-cell

Helper T-cell

phagocyte

bacterium

Studies showing the effect of this treatment in human patients wouldn't come for another 14 years. Allison spoke with 12 companies about the method, but no one was interested in backing it, in part because of previous failures with immunotherapy approaches to cancer treatment. But in 1998, the small biotech company Medarex bought the drug rights and made the human antibody to CTLA-4.

Ipilimumab blocks CTLA-4 to allow the T-cell to kill the cancer cell.

Setting the Car in Motion

Think of the immune system as similar to a car engine. There are two steps to setting a car in motion: turning the ignition and pressing on the gas pedal. To stop the car from moving, you press on the brake. The immune system functions in much the same way.

Most tumors, bacteria, and viruses produce a protein called an antigen. Antigen-presenting cells, a type of immune cell, capture the antigen and present it to T-cells. This starts the immune response; it turns the ignition. But a second interaction is needed before the T-cell is activated. As soon as this second interaction occurs, it's like pressing on the gas pedal—it sets the immune response in motion and the T-cell attacks the cancer cell. In some cases, however, the protein CTLA-4 prevents that second interaction from occurring, acting as a brake and interrupting the activation of the T-cell. One approach to cancer treatment is to block CTLA-4 so that the second signal occurs and T-cells can launch their attack.

One immunotherapy drug that functions this way is ipilimumab, an anti-CTLA-4 antibody produced by pharmaceutical company Medarex/Bristol-Myers Squibb. Bristol-Myers Squibb had purchased Medarex in 2009 and continued the clinical trials that were testing Allison's treatment approach. In 2010, they reported the results of a study that tested this drug in melanoma (skin cancer)

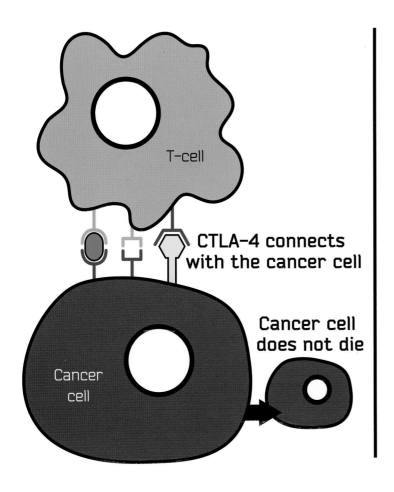

CTLA-4 connects
with the cancer cell

Cancer cell
does not die

Cancer
cell

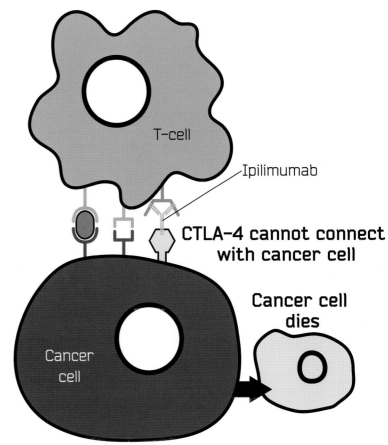

Ipilimumab

CTLA-4 cannot connect
with cancer cell

Cancer cell
dies

Cancer
cell

The Road Ahead

There have been many advances in cancer research. In general, the rate of death from cancer in the United States continues declining. This includes the most common types of cancer: lung, colon, breast, and prostate. One big step forward is curing acute lymphoblastic leukemia (ALL), the most common cancer diagnosed in children. ALL was once considered fatal.

Despite medical advances, cancer remains the second-leading cause of death in the United States after heart disease. More than 1.6 million new cancer cases are expected in the United States each year, and more than 500,000 Americans are expected to die from the disease.[5] The war on cancer is far from over.

patients whose cancers had relapsed and had no other treatment options. The researchers found patients who received the antibody lived an average of ten months. Patients who did not get the antibody lived for an average of six months. In some patients who received the antibody, the cancer disappeared altogether.

The US Food and Drug Administration (FDA) approved the drug for use in advanced melanoma patients a year later. Advanced-stage melanoma patients are expected to live seven months to a year, according to Allison. Long-term follow-up of the 5,000 patients who received the drug showed 22 percent survived for at least ten years, if not longer.[4] The results were astounding. Allison went on to win the 2014 Breakthrough Prize in Life Sciences for his discovery.

In immunotherapy, doctors remove blood from the body, treat it to increase or decrease the proportion of specific types of cells, and reinject it into the patient.

Another immunotherapy method involves genetically modifying a patient's T-cells to make them attack cancer cells directly, a method known as chimeric antigen receptor (CAR) therapy. This method is a type of gene therapy. In CAR therapy, T-cells are genetically modified to have proteins—the CARs—that recognize specific proteins on the cancer cells to target them. The modified T-cells are introduced into the patient, where they multiply and kill cancer cells, if all goes well. In 2013, researchers from the University of Pennsylvania and Memorial Sloan-Kettering Cancer Center in New York reported 45 out

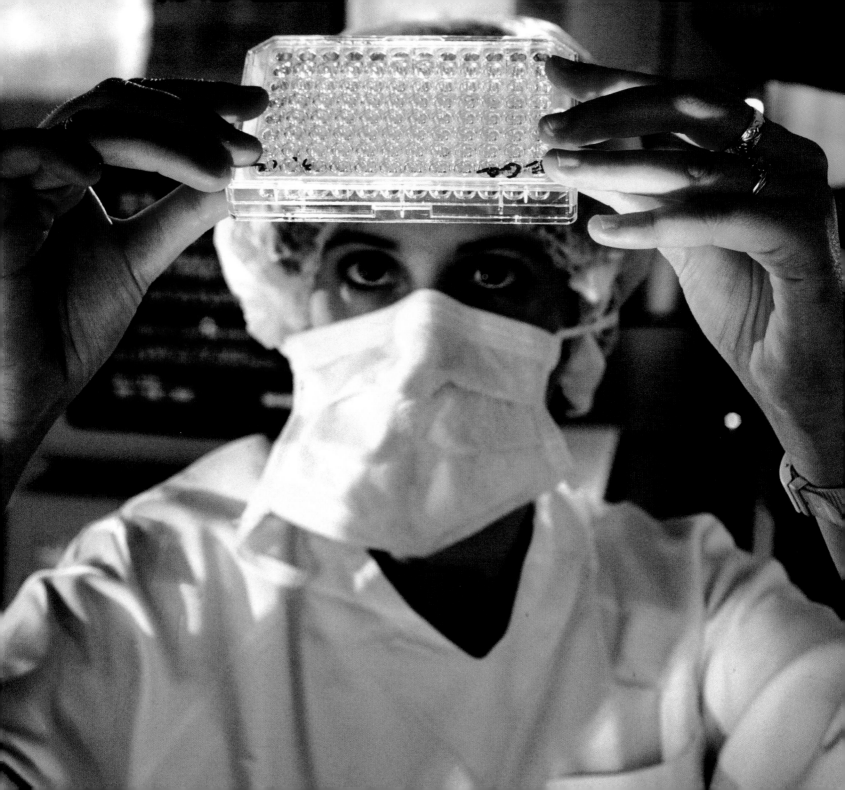

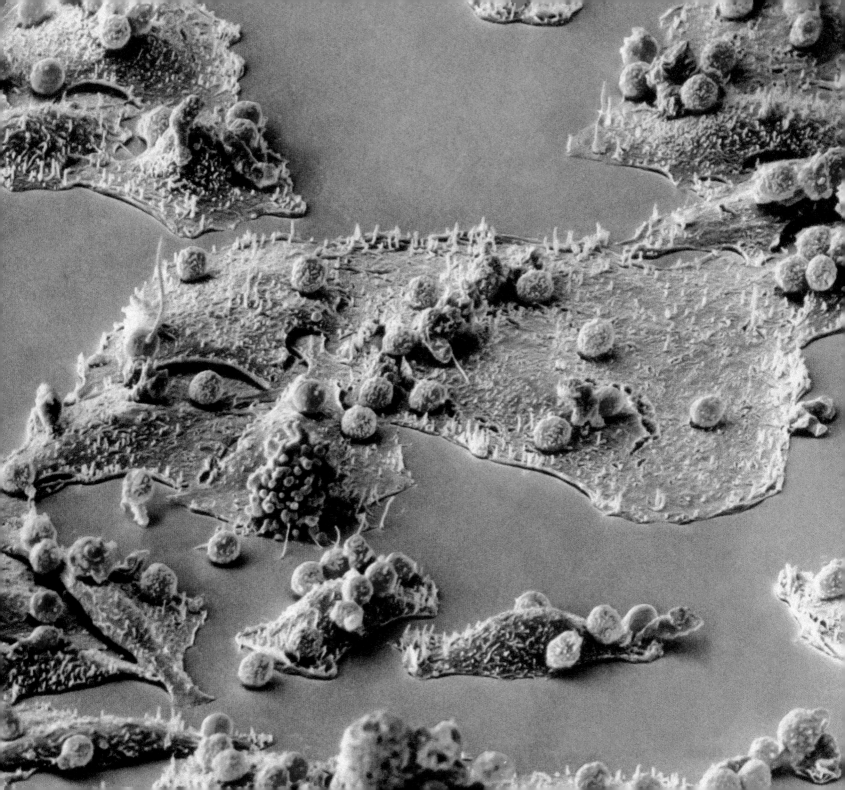

Immune cells, red, attack cancer cells, gray, as seen in a high-power microscope.

of 75 adults and children with leukemia who received CAR therapy went into complete remission, although some later relapsed. Another study published in late 2014 reported 23 of the 30 leukemia patients (both adults and children) who were treated with CAR therapy were alive six months after being treated. Nineteen of the 23 remained in remission when the article was published.

What's the Catch?

Immunotherapy does not work for every patient, and doctors have little understanding why. With other cancer treatments—surgery, radiation, or chemotherapy—it is typically clear right away whether the treatment worked or not. With immunotherapy, some tumors grow before vanishing. Patients may also experience severe side effects, such as inflammation of the colon. One major side effect is known as cytokine-release syndrome (CRS), which can produce a high fever, aches, low blood pressure, disorientation, and, in some cases, pulmonary edema, which is when fluid backs up in the lungs and causes shortness of breath. In several patients who received CAR T-cell therapy, CRS resulted in death.

Despite the current limitations and early false starts, immunotherapy has an extraordinary potential to change how cancer is treated. As *Science* magazine proclaimed in 2013, "For physicians accustomed to losing every patient with advanced disease, the numbers bring a hope they couldn't have fathomed a few years ago."[6] Unfortunately, the treatment doesn't work for every patient, and doctors are scrambling to find out why. But for the patients for whom the treatment is effective, immunotherapy has been an enormous success.

ZEROING IN ON
CANCER CELLS

The vast amount of research conducted has helped us better understand how cancer cells function. This knowledge has led scientists to develop new drugs that target certain cancer cell qualities, such as their ability to replicate or develop a blood supply that brings oxygen and nutrients.

Although conventional cancer drugs used during chemotherapy target cancer cells, they also affect healthy cells. This is why most of these drugs have unpleasant side effects. As the American Cancer Society explains, "Cancer cells tend to grow fast, and chemo drugs kill fast-growing cells. But because these drugs travel throughout the body, they can affect normal, healthy cells that are fast-growing too."[1] The normal, fast-growing cells most likely to be damaged are hair follicles, blood-forming cells in bone marrow, cells in the mouth and the digestive system, and reproductive cells. This is why many patients experience hair loss and nausea. By targeting specific cancer cell characteristics

Researchers around the world are at work on better cancer drugs that target tumors more precisely.

How Magic Bullets Operate

In many cases the immune system does not recognize cancer cells as foreign substances, so it does not attack them. Some monoclonal antibodies make cancer cells more visible to patients' immune cells. When a monoclonal antibody attaches to a specific part of a cancer cell, the cell is flagged so the immune system can find it.

Other monoclonal antibodies prevent new blood vessels from forming around cancer cells. Without a blood supply, the cells die. Still other monoclonal antibodies block growth factor receptors on cancer cells. Growth factors tell cells to grow and multiply. Cancer cells tend to have more of these receptors than normal cells, which is why they grow so fast. Blocking these receptors can slow or stop their growth.

Some monoclonal antibodies carry radioactive particles or chemotherapy drugs. They deliver radiation or drug therapies directly to cancer cells without damaging surrounding cells.

instead, researchers hope to destroy the cancer cells while reducing traditional side effects.

Monoclonal antibodies, blue, will only attach to a specific antigen on a cell, gold.

Anticancer Antibodies

One method of targeting cancer cells uses naturally occurring or man-made antibodies. Antibodies used to treat cancer are known as monoclonal antibodies. *Mono* means single and *clonal* refers to cloning, or making exact copies of something. Scientists create monoclonal antibodies by cloning a single immune cell that targets a single antigen. Monoclonal antibodies used against cancer attach to specific parts of cancer cells.

According to a 2012 article in the journal *Cancer Immunity*, "Monoclonal antibody-based treatment of cancer has been established as one of the most successful therapeutic strategies for both [blood] malignancies and solid tumors in the last 20 years."[2] Indeed, many doctors refer to monoclonal antibodies as "magic bullets," though they do have side effects.[3]

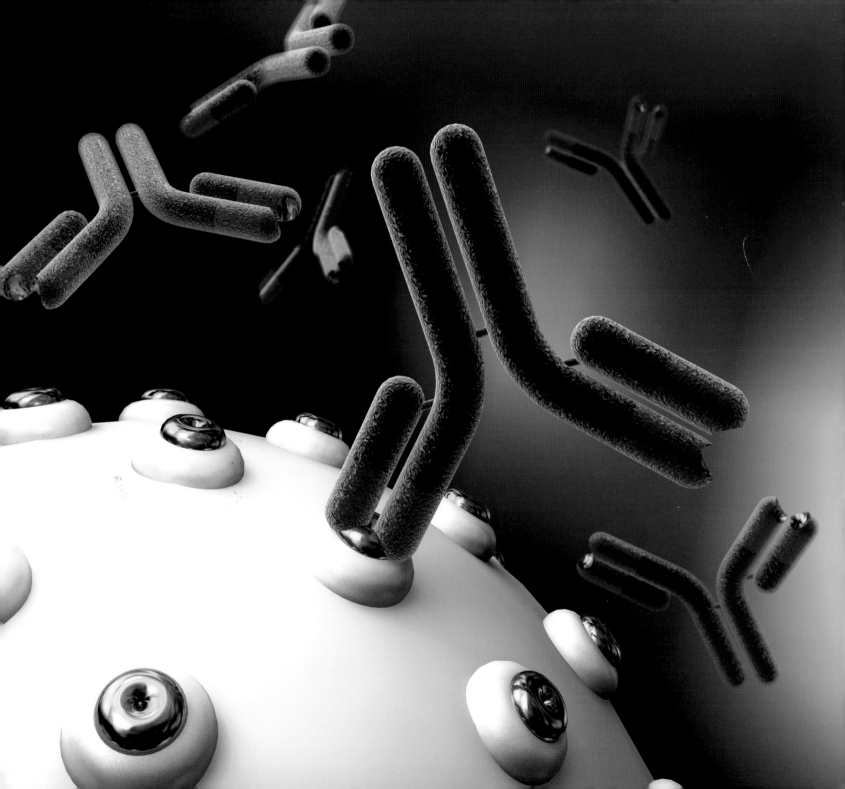

One widely used monoclonal antibody is trastuzumab, sold under the brand name Herceptin. Herceptin attaches to cancer cells called HER2 positive cells, which have more HER2 receptors than normal. HER2 receptors signal cells to grow and multiply. But cells with too many HER2 receptors grow too quickly. Herceptin blocks these growth signals. Because Herceptin targets HER2 receptors, doctors perform laboratory tests for these receptors on tumor samples before prescribing the drug.

Smuggling Drugs into Cancer Cells

Researchers are testing monoclonal antibodies for a different type of targeted therapy, called antibody directed enzyme prodrug therapy (ADEPT). First scientists attach an enzyme to an antibody that targets a particular cancer cell antigen. The enzyme's job is to activate a prodrug, or an inactive drug, that needs to react with the enzyme in order to work. After the antibody-enzyme combination is injected into a patient, the antibody heads for the patient's cancer cells. The antibodies bind to the cancer cells, where the enzyme activates the prodrug. This process ensures the active drug is released only in the presence of the cancer cells, which decreases the potential damage to the rest of the body.

Although scientists have been experimenting with ADEPT since the 1980s, no ADEPT treatment drugs have been approved. According to a 2014 study by researchers led by Dr. Roger Harrison at the University of Oklahoma, "Enzyme prodrug therapy shows promise for the treatment of solid tumors, but current approaches lack effective/safe delivery strategies."[4] The study did make progress in delivery methods. The researchers found that putting together three different enzymes with several prostate cancer prodrugs killed 60 to 99 percent of patients' cancer cells without significantly damaging other cells. Scientists believe this method should be tested further.

Sneaking Drugs into Cells with Vitamins

Small molecule drug conjugates (SMDCs) are another new method of zeroing in on cancer cells. Conjugates are substances that are linked together. SMDCs operate similarly to antibody-enzyme combinations, but they use small molecules instead of antibodies. Small molecules are typically vitamins or nutrients that tumors specifically need.

SMDCs contain three components: a targeting ligand, or a molecule that binds to another molecule; a linker; and a powerful, toxic drug that kills cancer cells. The drug is too toxic to give patients unless it is specifically targeted to cancer cells. The targeting ligand gets the drug into cancer cells. The linker releases the drug only after the cancer cells take up the SMDC. According to the biopharmaceutical company Endocyte, which is developing several SMDCs to treat cancer, this targeted approach allows doctors to use drugs that are "thousands of times more active than traditional cancer-killing drugs."[5]

◢ What are Prodrugs?

Prodrugs are inactive drugs that are converted to active drugs once they get inside a patient's body. Some are activated by chemicals within the body. Others must come into contact with an enzyme designed to recognize and activate the prodrug. Doctors use prodrugs for several reasons. Prodrugs can last longer than always-active drugs. Prodrugs can also be targeted to cancer cells by monoclonal antibody-enzyme combinations, thereby protecting body cells from the effects of toxic prodrugs. Prodrugs may also be used because the active form of the drug may be unable to enter the organ in which it is needed. For example, the prodrug levodopa is used to treat Parkinson's disease, which is caused by a lack of the brain chemical dopamine. Dopamine cannot cross into the brain from the bloodstream, but levodopa can. Once levodopa is inside the brain, a brain protein called dopa decarboxylase converts it to the active form of dopamine.

One SMDC Endocyte is testing is vintafolide. Its targeted ligand is folic acid, the synthetic form of the B vitamin folate. Since cancer cells multiply rapidly, they must frequently copy their DNA. Folate is essential for this process. That's why some types of cancer cells have many more folate receptors than other cells. Thus the cancer cells take up more of the vintafolide than other cells, reducing the drug's overall toxic effects on the rest of the body. Some clinical trials indicate vintafolide is effective in treating ovarian cancer. Other studies, however, show no positive effects. Testing on this promising drug continues.

Nasty (and Useful) Viruses

Viruses that cause diseases are usually considered the enemy. But some of these microorganisms offer another promising method of targeting and killing many types of cancer cells.

Researchers at Duke University are conducting clinical trials using a genetically engineered poliovirus (PVS-RIPO) against a brain cancer called glioblastoma. Poliovirus causes polio, a contagious disease that causes paralysis. Polio affected thousands of Americans before the first polio vaccine became available in 1955. Duke researchers chose poliovirus as a cancer-killing agent because most cancer cells contain poliovirus receptors. PVS-RIPO therefore readily enters cancer cells. It cannot cause polio in patients because the scientists inserted a piece of DNA from a different virus into the poliovirus genome, disrupting its ability to make people sick.

The Duke team has found when they inject PVS-RIPO directly into brain tumors, it selectively enters and kills tumor cells by causing them to burst. It also stimulates patients' immune systems to attack the tumor. The immune system activation occurs because the immune system responds quickly to the presence of viruses. PVS-RIPO does not kill normal cells because it is engineered to multiply inside

How Small Molecule Drug Conjugates Work

(1) The small molecule drug conjugate (SMDC) consists of a small molecule attached to a toxin by a linker. (2) They are injected into the patient. They bind to receptors on cancer cells. (3) The receptor pulls the SMDC inside the cancer cell. (4) Inside, the toxin releases and the cell is killed.

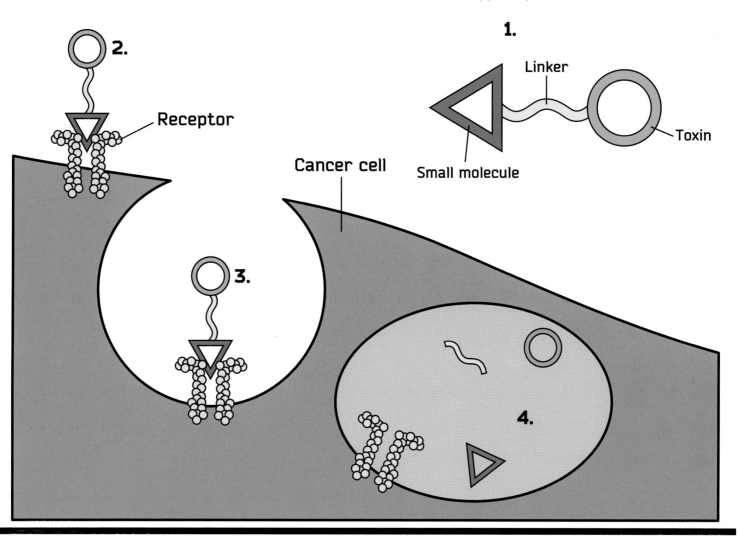

Camel and Alpaca Antibodies to the Rescue

Using viruses that enter cancer cells through naturally occurring cancer cell receptors is just one method scientists are testing for getting viruses into cancer cells. Another method involves connecting a virus to an antibody that is engineered to target specific cancer cells. One challenge with making effective virus-antibody compounds is that human antibodies and those of most animals cannot survive outside cells. Therefore, when a virus-antibody complex enters a cancer cell and the virus multiplies and causes the cell to burst, the antibody falls apart before it can get to other cancer cells. In February 2015, scientists at Washington University School of Medicine led by Dr. David Curiel announced they found a potential solution to this problem. Camel and alpaca antibodies have a sturdier shape than most antibodies. They can survive outside cells. The researchers attached camel or alpaca antibodies to viruses and placed these compounds into laboratory dishes containing cancer cells. After cells began bursting and releasing virus-antibody compounds, the antibodies continued targeting other cells. The next step is to try this in laboratory animals.

cancer cells only. It replicates so much it causes cancer cells to burst and die. This new targeted therapy, along with other ways of zeroing in on cancer cells, offers cancer patients new hope.

The poliovirus is encased in proteins that protect it from heat and acid.

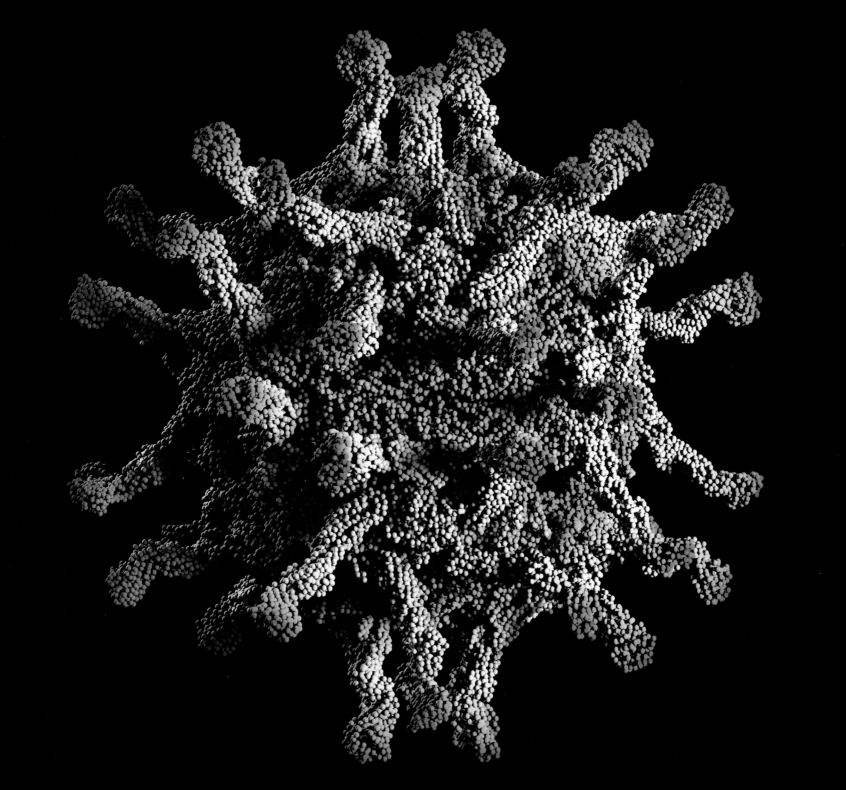

FOUR

GENETICS AND PERSONALIZED MEDICINE

M edications can function differently in different patients. While a specific drug might be effective for one patient, another patient may experience significant side effects or the drug may not be effective at all. For years, health-care providers have been increasing their focus on treating individual patients rather than the disease itself. Today, researchers are determining ways to target therapies specifically to a patient's genetic makeup, health history, and environment.

In his State of the Union address on January 20, 2015, President Barack Obama unveiled a new initiative to fund research for personalized medicine. A White House press release reported, "The Precision Medicine Initiative will pioneer a new model of patient-powered research that promises

A procedure called genetic sequencing can discover a person's unique genetic code.

The Backbone of Personalized Medicine

One of the biggest advances in modern scientific research was the first sequence of the human genome in 2003. It was a result of the Human Genome Project, which was a collaboration of scientists from around the world. The sequence took 13 years to discover and cost $3 billion.[3] Due to improving technology, it was possible in 2015 to map an individual's genome in a matter of hours for approximately $1,000.[4] When the first draft of the sequence was released in 2000, US President Bill Clinton remarked: "Without a doubt, this is the most important, most wondrous map ever produced by humankind."[5]

to . . . provide clinicians with new tools, knowledge, and therapies to select which treatments will work best for which patients."[1]

Approximately half of the $215 million investment will be given to a new research group that aims to collect data from 1 million or more volunteers—data that includes medical records, lab tests, and genetic profiles—to develop new tools and drugs to combat diseases. Seventy million dollars will go to the National Cancer Institute to conduct research on genes that may contribute to developing certain types of cancer.[2] The FDA will also receive funding to develop databases and regulations to protect privacy and support public health. Developers of the initiative say a one-size-fits-all approach to medical care is outdated, and it's necessary to recognize the importance of individualized care.

Electronic medical records help reduce errors and make one person's records easily accessible to doctors in different locations.

Immediate results are unlikely. It will take years to collect genomic data from a million people and develop new diagnostic tests and treatments based on this data. But it is a significant step forward in advancing personalized medicine.

Personal Information

Name

Gender   ○ Male   ○ Female

Date of Birth

Marital Status   ○ Single   ○ Married
                      ○ Widowed   ○ Divorced

Nationality

Occupation

Address

Telephone number

e-mail address

[Previous] [Done] [Next] [Exit]

EMR System

Personal Information

Social Information

Insurance

Diagnosis

Treatment

Medical History

Healthcare Calendar

Schedule

Appointment

Personalized Medicine Gains Celebrity Status

Actress Angelina Jolie, who lost her mother, a grandmother, and an aunt to cancer, is a poster child for personalized approaches to cancer prevention. After genetic testing revealed Jolie carried an inherited mutation in the BRCA1 gene, doctors informed her she had an 87 percent risk of developing breast cancer and a 50 percent risk of developing ovarian cancer. In 2013, Jolie made the decision to have a preventive double mastectomy, having both breasts removed to minimize the risk of cancer. After her surgery, her risk of developing breast cancer dropped from 87 percent to less than five percent.[7] In 2015, she was told there was a chance she was showing signs of early ovarian cancer. Although further testing revealed she did not have cancerous tumors, Jolie opted to have her ovaries removed to reduce her future risk. Studies have shown that since Jolie went public with her decision, more women are choosing to receive genetic testing for BRCA1 mutations. There have also been many more inquiries into risk-reducing mastectomies.

Combining Drugs for Better Results

Because different peoples' genetic makeup makes them respond differently to medications, one method of personalizing medicine is to administer combinations of drugs that work best for a particular individual. In addition, the genotype, or genetic makeup, of viruses or other disease-causing microorganisms may also dictate which drug combinations are most effective. For example, the liver disease chronic hepatitis C, which affects approximately 2.7 million people and kills 15,000 each year in the United States, is caused by the hepatitis C virus.[6] Scientists have identified at least six hepatitis C virus genotypes and more than 50 virus subtypes. Knowing the virus genotype helps doctors predict how well a patient will respond to treatment. It also helps determine how long treatment should last. The FDA approved a new drug combination for treating hepatitis C in December 2013. The new combination removes one drug with many side effects and replaces it with one that has few side effects.

A Drug Made to Order

Another method of personalizing medicine involves using drugs that target specific gene mutations responsible for a patient's illness. In 2008, researchers at the Dana-Farber Cancer Institute reported the successful use of a targeted drug to treat a melanoma patient whose cancer was metastatic. Lab tests revealed the tumor cells of the 79-year-old patient had a mutation in a gene called *KIT*. The patient was enrolled in a trial in which she received the drug Imatinib, marketed as Gleevec, which specifically targets that gene. The drug works by blocking an enzyme that is stuck in the "on" position, causing out-of-control cell growth. One month later, two of her tumors had disappeared, and the other tumors had reduced in size. Nine months after the study, she remained in stable condition.

Two years later, a targeted drug used to treat the same condition was found to be effective in more than 80 percent of patients enrolled in a clinical trial.[8] Since that time, targeted therapies have been used to treat a wide variety of illnesses and cancers.

Gene Therapy

Gene therapy—an experimental technique that uses a patient's genes to treat or prevent disease—may someday allow doctors to treat diseases by inserting a gene into a patient's cells, effectively rewriting their DNA. The technique remains risky because it is not effective in every patient and in some cases can be fatal. In the 2010s, it is only being tested for the treatment of diseases with no other cures, such as certain advanced cancers. The concept of gene therapy has been around for decades. Despite significant setbacks in the 1990s, the technique has been gaining momentum in recent years.

Gene therapy gained attention from the medical community in the 1980s and 1990s. In 1980, two Stanford researchers, Richard Mulligan and Paul Berg, published a paper in the journal *Science*.

They reported they had used gene therapy to treat Lesch-Nyhan syndrome (LNS), a rare inherited childhood disease. LNS causes a range of symptoms including arthritis and a compulsion to self-mutilate, including behaviors such as biting or head banging. The paper caught the attention of researcher James Wilson, who was studying LNS at the University of Michigan. The findings inspired him to devote his career to developing gene therapy as a method to treat inherited diseases such as LNS.

Wilson studied the use of viruses to carry genes into human cells to repair their DNA. He focused on the adenovirus, which causes the common cold. Wilson engineered the virus so it could deliver genes without infecting the patient or causing any cold symptoms. In 1999, Wilson supported a trial that tested whether this method was safe. The subjects were 18 patients with ornithine transcarbamylase (OTC) deficiency, a rare genetic disorder that causes ammonia to collect in the blood. Ammonia levels that are too high can be toxic.

Copies of OTC genes that didn't have the defect were delivered inside the adenovirus and injected into the patients' blood. But in one 18-year-old patient, Jesse Gelsinger, the virus led to massive organ failure. Gelsinger died three days later.

Gelsinger's death prompted an investigation into the study. The investigation found there were previous studies in monkeys that had also produced negative effects, but they had not been clearly communicated. Wilson was banned from conducting human clinical trials for five years, and the field of gene therapy nearly came to a close.

In recent years, however, researchers have reported successes in using gene therapy to treat cancer and other diseases. In 2012, a gene therapy drug called Glybera was approved for commercial use by the European Medicines Agency, marking the first time a gene therapy has been made available for the

Viral Shapes

Viruses come in a variety of shapes. The adenovirus Wilson used is polyhedral.

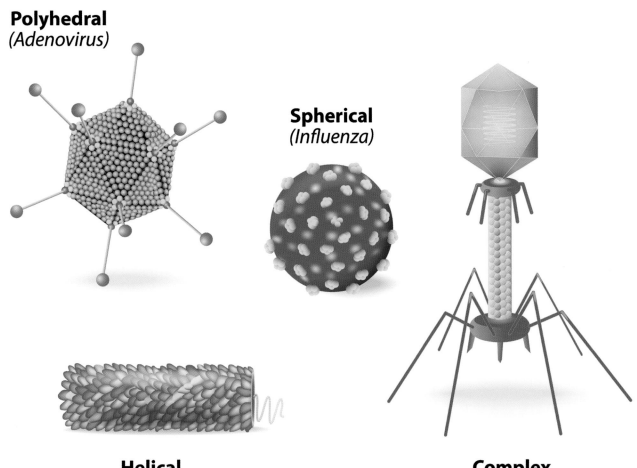

Polyhedral
(Adenovirus)

Spherical
(Influenza)

Helical
(Tobacco mosaic virus)

Complex
(Bacteriophage)

Genetics Ethics and Henrietta Lacks

In 1951, Henrietta Lacks, a 31-year-old cervical cancer patient, died in a Baltimore, Maryland, hospital. Before her death, doctors removed some of her tumor cells. It was determined these cells could grow and thrive inside a lab without dying off. Her cells, named HeLa cells, have since been used in thousands of experiments, furthering our understanding of vaccines, developing new treatments for cancer, and spurring numerous scientific advances. But Lacks never consented to this use of her cells. In 2013, a European research team sparked an ethical controversy when it published Lacks's genome without the consent of her family. Lacks's family ultimately reached an agreement with researchers about the use of her genetic data, but the issue raised ethical concerns about regulations around sharing genetic data.

public outside of clinical trials. Glybera is used to treat lipoprotein lipase deficiency, a rare genetic disorder that prevents patients from breaking down fat from digested food.

But discovering and testing new gene therapies is expensive. Gene therapy is often used to treat very rare disorders, so pharmaceutical companies are unlikely to make a profit even if the drug becomes available to the public. Reports published in 2015 revealed Glybera would cost close to $1 million per treatment when it went on sale in Germany.[9]

Personalized medicine is gaining popularity as researchers learn more about genetic conditions and develop therapies to treat them. Organizations including the Personal Genome Project, headed by George Church of Harvard Medical School, seek to compile genetic data on as many people as possible to help researchers find patterns and refine treatments. It is likely personalized medicine will become the standard of care not only for genetic disorders but also for routine care. Diagnoses and treatments are currently being developed in response to an incoming wealth of medical data.

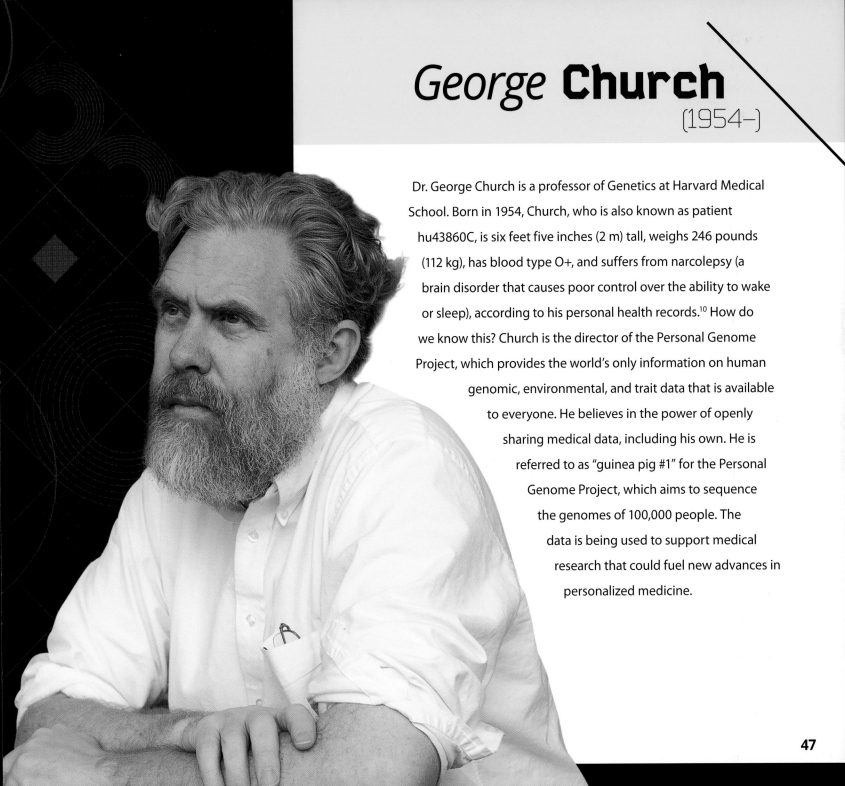

George **Church**

(1954–)

Dr. George Church is a professor of Genetics at Harvard Medical School. Born in 1954, Church, who is also known as patient hu43860C, is six feet five inches (2 m) tall, weighs 246 pounds (112 kg), has blood type O+, and suffers from narcolepsy (a brain disorder that causes poor control over the ability to wake or sleep), according to his personal health records.[10] How do we know this? Church is the director of the Personal Genome Project, which provides the world's only information on human genomic, environmental, and trait data that is available to everyone. He believes in the power of openly sharing medical data, including his own. He is referred to as "guinea pig #1" for the Personal Genome Project, which aims to sequence the genomes of 100,000 people. The data is being used to support medical research that could fuel new advances in personalized medicine.

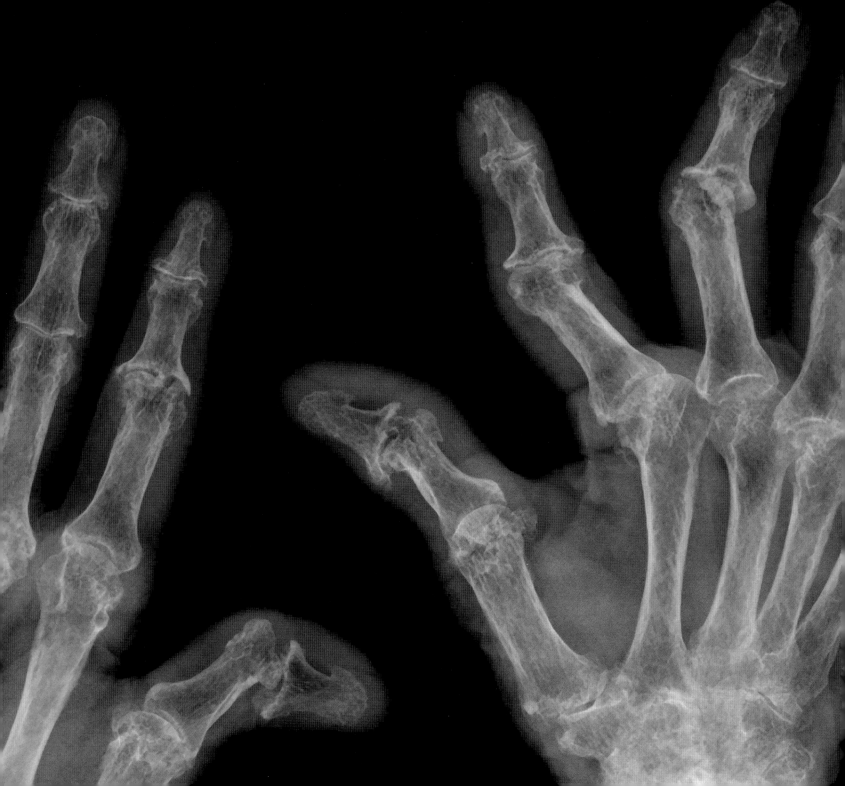

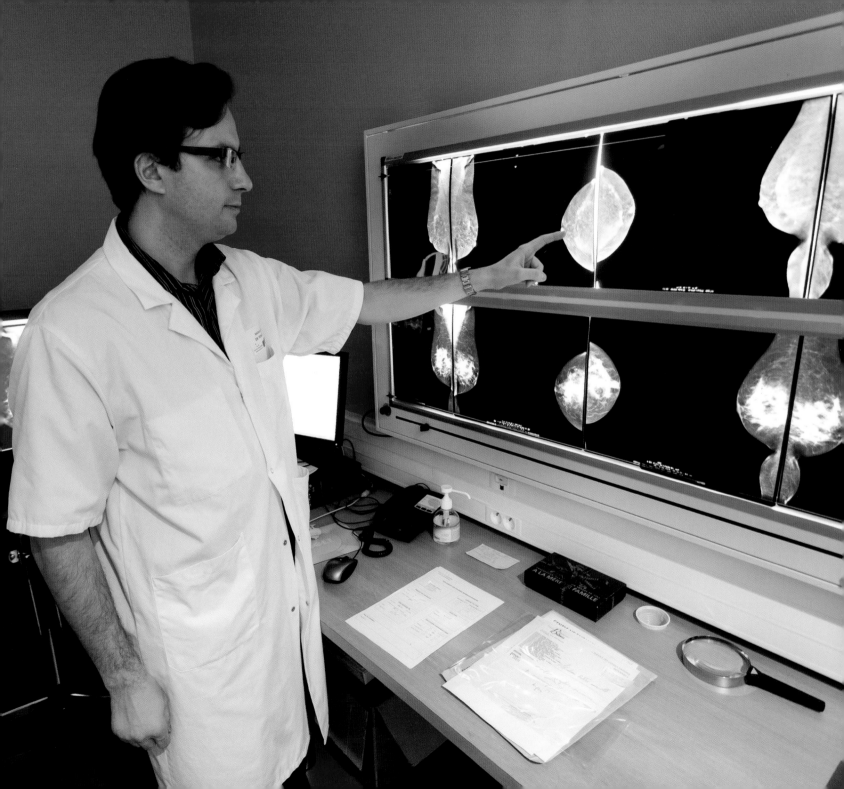

a 15 percent drop in the recall rate, meaning fewer women were brought back for additional screening because of false alarms.[3]

Current two-dimensional mammography uses side-to-side and top-to-bottom X rays of the breast. This type of mammography can sometimes create shadows that look like cancer, which can result in patients who don't actually have cancer getting called back for additional screening and tests. In addition, two-dimensional mammograms sometimes fail to detect cancer tumors that are hiding behind normal tissue. With three-dimensional mammography, which was approved by the FDA in 2011, X-ray images are taken in an arc across the breast, collecting pictures from multiple angles. A computer program then develops a stack of thin layers a radiologist can read, much like the pages of a book. Millions of American women receive three-dimensional mammograms each year. The number is likely to continue increasing due to the success of the new technology. But the three-dimensional machines are much more expensive than the standard two-dimensional machines, which may prevent some health facilities from investing in the equipment until more research is published.

Google and medical company Novartis are partnering on developing a contact lens that can detect blood sugar levels for diabetics.

A Potential Cure for Diabetes

In 2015, more than 25 million people in the United States had diabetes. According to the US Centers for Disease Control and Prevention, more than a quarter of them are undiagnosed.[4] Type 1 diabetes is a chronic condition in which the pancreas produces little or no insulin, which is a hormone the body needs to allow glucose to enter cells and produce energy. Type 1 diabetes accounts for approximately 5 percent of diabetes cases. It is often diagnosed in children and young adults.[5] There is no known way to prevent it. Type 2 diabetes, which accounts for about 95 percent of diabetes cases, occurs when the body becomes resistant to insulin or doesn't produce enough.[6] This usually occurs over time and is

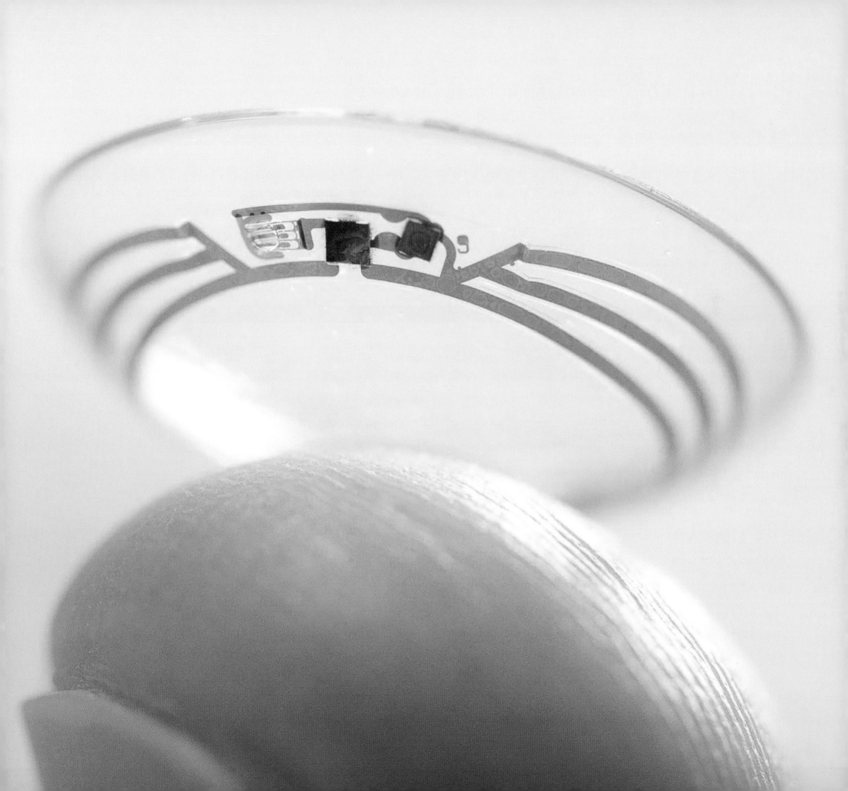

A Pill to Prevent All Chronic Diseases?

In 2014, researchers from the United Kingdom published the results of a study comparing two drugs used to treat type 2 diabetes, metformin and sulphonylurea, to see which one helped elderly people with diabetes live longer. The researchers also included a group of nondiabetics to compare against the people receiving the drugs. They found that people with diabetes who took metformin lived longer than those who took sulphonylurea. But there was another interesting finding. People with diabetes (who were between 71 and 75 when the study began) who took metformin also lived longer than the people who didn't have diabetes who hadn't received any drug. The results left other researchers wondering if this drug could actually prevent other diseases associated with aging, such as Alzheimer's disease, heart disease, or even cancer. A new trial is looking at the effect of metformin on delaying or preventing other chronic diseases.

mostly diagnosed in people who are overweight or obese. Increased body fat makes it harder for the body to use insulin in the right way.

People with type 1 diabetes must closely monitor their blood sugar and take insulin for their whole lives. But breakthrough research offered these patients a ray of hope in late 2014. Harvard researchers announced they were able to produce large quantities of beta cells, the cells that are used to produce insulin, for the first time by using human embryonic stem cells.

Doug Melton, the study's lead scientist, has a personal stake in the research. Melton's son was diagnosed with type 1 diabetes as an infant, and his daughter was diagnosed with the same disease at age 14. He has devoted his life's work to finding a cure for the disease. Creating huge numbers of the cells that are missing in people with diabetes was a significant step toward this goal. The next step is ensuring the immune system does not reject the cells once they are implanted in a patient.

In the meantime, the cells may be able to treat people with type 2 diabetes who depend on insulin shots. Unlike type 1 diabetes, which is an immune system disorder, the bodies of people with type 2 diabetes would not destroy the beta cells. The cells are a temporary fix, however, and patients must modify their lifestyle and diet to continue the benefits of the treatment. The discovery was near the top of the list for the *Science* Breakthrough of the Year award in 2014.

These are just a few examples of scientific advances that help to prevent, screen for, and treat chronic diseases, which account for 84 percent of US health-care costs each year.[7] Experts expect the incidence of chronic diseases to increase in the future since people are living longer than ever before. In 1900, the average life expectancy in the United States was 46 years.[8] In 2012, it was 78.8 years.[9] The Council on Social Work Education explains, "Although chronic diseases affect people of all ages, the risk of chronic illness increases with age, and people aged 65 years or older are more apt to have multiple chronic illnesses."[10] Given the rapid aging of the US population, doctors and patients will increasingly rely on new technologies to address these chronic illnesses.

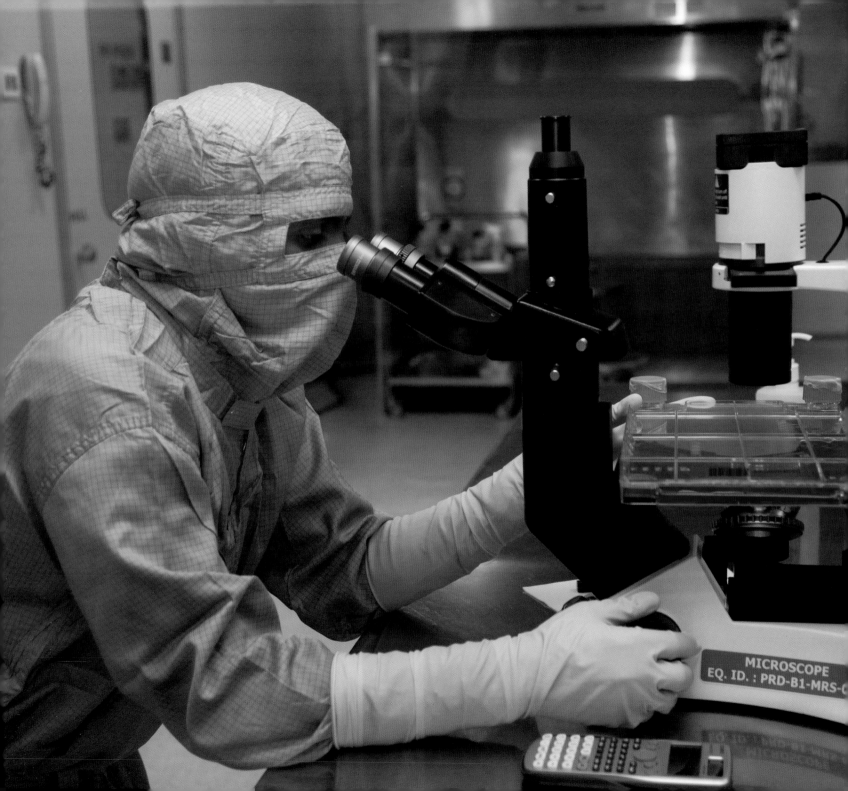

MICROSCOPE
EQ. ID. : PRD-B1-MRS-C

SIX

ADVANCES AND CHALLENGES IN
VACCINE RESEARCH

Humans live in an increasingly connected society, which can mean infectious diseases have the potential to spread rapidly. But human connectedness also spurs the development of innovative technologies to attack these diseases, including vaccines. Vaccines are the cheapest and most effective way to prevent disease in the world. Millions of infections are prevented each year because of existing vaccines. But some diseases continue to elude researchers who are struggling to develop effective vaccines and therapies to combat them. In other cases, existing vaccines and therapies are being underused. ○

A new and affordable vaccine developed in India prevents diarrhea caused by the rotavirus and will save millions of children's lives.

Vaccine Panic

From January 1, 2015, to June 26, 2015, 178 people across 24 states and Washington, DC, reported having measles. Many of those who caught the disease had never been vaccinated. Most of these cases were part of a multistate outbreak that began at an amusement park in California. In 2014, the United States experienced 23 measles outbreaks, including one that caused 383 cases within communities where people were largely unvaccinated.[1] Why were so many people not getting the vaccine, which is recommended for all children? Concerns about vaccine safety dates back to the time the very first vaccine was developed. But it was in 1998 when a researcher at the Royal Free Hospital in London published a paper concluding the measles, mumps, and rubella (MMR) vaccine might have a relationship to the onset of autism, a condition that includes a range of developmental disorders in the brain. Although the paper was later retracted by the journal, as it was based on faulty evidence, and the researcher's medical license was revoked, the damage was done. Anti-vaccine groups emerged around the world. Despite a wealth of scientific evidence demonstrating vaccines have no link to autism, the controversy continues.

How Do Vaccines Work?

When confronted by bacteria or a virus, the body's immune system kicks into gear to fight off the infection. It deploys immune cells to identify the foreign invader and attack it. After the infection has passed, the body's immune cells retain memory of their encounter. Known as memory immune cells, these cells go quickly into action if the infection comes back to eliminate it immediately.

Vaccines imitate a natural infection so the body will create these memory immune cells. For example, the yellow fever vaccine contains a very weak form of the virus that doesn't cause an infection but instead prompts the immune system to produce its response so that it will retain the memory cells.

Vaccine Upsides and Downsides

The recommended annual vaccinations that are given to children around the world have helped prevent 3 million deaths each year.[2] Vaccines helped eliminate smallpox and have nearly eliminated polio. Vaccines have had a substantial effect on reducing the numbers of infections for measles, pertussis (also known as whooping cough), yellow fever, and many other diseases.

Despite advances in vaccine research, there are a number of diseases that still don't have effective vaccines. Human immunodeficiency virus (HIV), malaria, dengue fever, tuberculosis, and influenza cause nearly 4 million deaths each year globally, and currently there are no good vaccines to prevent them.[3] Tuberculosis and influenza do have vaccines, but they have a limited effect on patients.

The First Vaccine

The first vaccine was developed in 1796 by Edward Jenner, a doctor living in England, to combat smallpox. Smallpox caused a rash and fever, and sometimes death. Jenner had noticed that milkmaids infected with cowpox—a viral disease of cows' udders that resembles a mild case smallpox when contracted by humans—seemed to be immune to outbreaks of smallpox. Jenner took pus from a cowpox lesion on a milkmaid's hand and applied it under the skin of an eight-year-old boy's arm. He then infected this boy with smallpox, but the boy was immune to the disease. Later vaccine development refined the method. Today, smallpox is considered extinct because of successful worldwide vaccination.

What's the Holdup?

Part of the issue with developing vaccines for these diseases is that they don't function the same way in the body as other vaccine-preventable diseases do. For example, there is limited understanding of how the immune system responds to infection from malaria parasites. For most vaccines, the immune

HIV Life Cycle

HIV reproduces by attaching and fusing to cells. Its DNA is changed so it can integrate into the cell's DNA. Then the cell assembles new viruses.

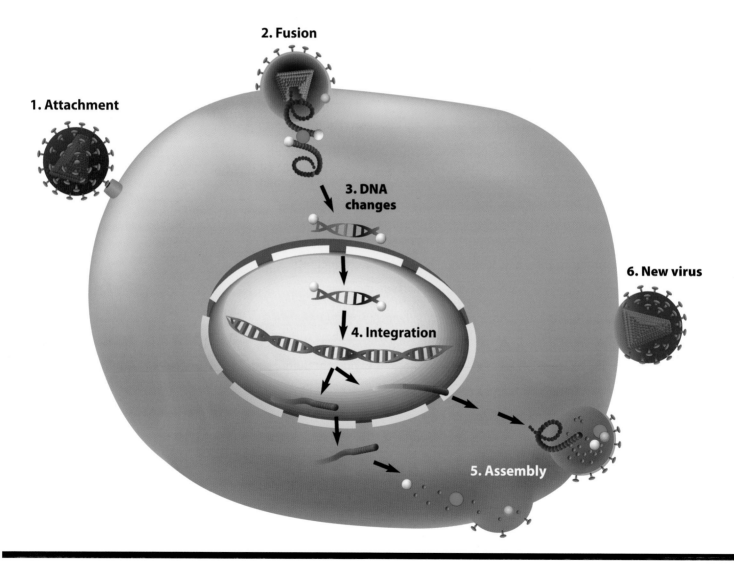

1. Attachment

2. Fusion

3. DNA changes

4. Integration

5. Assembly

6. New virus

system offers lifelong protection once the infection has been cleared. But one bout of malaria only partially protects against future infections. A person might receive a second or third malaria infection but experience milder symptoms. In addition, malaria parasites mutate rapidly, quickly becoming immune to any vaccine.

HIV infects and destroys T-cells. When these cells fall below a certain level, patients are highly vulnerable to life-threatening conditions. This is when an HIV patient is diagnosed with acquired immune deficiency syndrome (AIDS). HIV presents a problem for vaccine development. HIV infects and destroys T-cells, the immune cells responsible for coordinating the immune response. Therefore, activating T-cells with a vaccine is a huge challenge. Scientists haven't found any cases of people who have completely recovered from HIV, so they can't look at an example of a successful immune response and try to mimic it. And once a person is infected with HIV, the virus mutates and develops new strains. A vaccine would have to protect against multiple strains of the virus.

Reducing HIV Risk

In the absence of an HIV vaccine, scientists have been studying other methods for preventing HIV infection. One effective method is called pre-exposure prophylaxis, or PrEP. PrEP is a method of treating people who do not have HIV but are at high risk of getting it. This method is most often recommended for people who are in ongoing relationships with HIV-infected partners, people who do not use condoms during sex when they don't know of their partners HIV status, or people who inject drugs and might share injection equipment. PrEP involves taking a pill once per day. If taken consistently, it can reduce the risk of HIV in these high-risk groups by up to 92 percent.[4] Recommendations for the use of PrEP in the United States were released in 2014.

Malaria: Room for Hope

According to research results released in April 2015, a malaria vaccine that has been in development for more than 20 years is partially effective. Researchers report that over a three to four year period, the vaccine prevented a large number of cases when given to infants and small children. To be most effective, the vaccine requires three shots within three months and then a booster shot a year and a half later. The researchers concluded, "The vaccine has the potential to make a substantial contribution to malaria control when used in combination with other effective control measures."[5] The new vaccine should not be considered a solution on its own. It should be given alongside a host of other prevention strategies, such as mosquito nets and indoor insecticide spraying.

With more than 500,000 children under five dying each year from malaria, even a partially effective vaccine could make an enormous impact.[6] However, it is unfortunately less effective in infants than in small children ages one to five, and it doesn't protect against severe malaria in infants. Needing a booster shot also lessens the vaccine's effectiveness. In developing countries, traveling to a health facility for vaccinations can be costly and time-consuming. It can be difficult for parents or caregivers to be able to take more time off of work and spend money to travel to get a booster shot.

Malaria parasites, red, multiply inside red blood cells, purple, causing the cells to burst.

Cancer Vaccines: Prevention and Treatment

Researchers have developed vaccines that prevent some cancers caused by viruses or other microorganisms. The vaccines Gardasil and Cervarix prevent cervical cancer and other cancers caused by several types of human papillomaviruses, which cause warts that in some cases can become cancerous. These vaccines contain virus proteins that are targeted by the recipient's immune system.

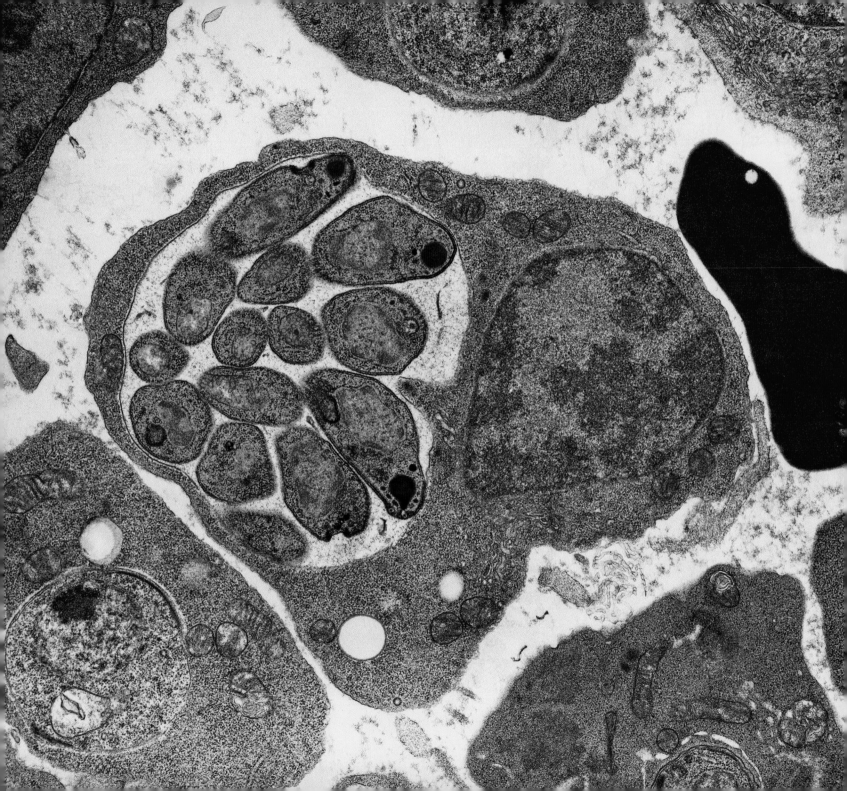

Another cancer-preventing vaccine is the hepatitis B vaccine. This prevents hepatitis B, which is a leading cause of liver cancer.

Most vaccines are used to prevent diseases. But some cancer vaccines are intended for disease treatment. There is only one approved vaccine to treat cancer: Provenge, used to treat men with metastatic prostate cancer. The manufacturer makes each dose for a specific patient by combining immune cells from the patient's blood with antigens from prostate cancer cells. Doctors then give the vaccine in three doses. Clinical trials indicate Provenge stimulates the immune system to attack cancer cells, helping patients live four months longer on average. But custom-making each dose is expensive—the cost of treatment is $93,000.[7] Many insurance companies and some governments with national health care, such as the United Kingdom, will not pay for Provenge because they believe the cost is not worth the expected benefit.

Researchers are developing other preventive and treatment vaccines for many cancers. As scientists gain new knowledge about how cancer cells influence the immune system, more effective vaccines can be made.

Gene Therapy Vaccination

In February 2015, researchers from Scripps Research Institute published a study showing a form of gene therapy was effective in eliminating the equivalent of HIV from monkeys and preventing future infections. The technique is being tested for a range of diseases, including malaria, influenza, and hepatitis, all of which have eluded vaccine scientists for years.

This gene therapy method, called immunoprophylaxis by gene transfer, or I.G.T., creates artificial versions of genes that produce antibodies to fight the specific disease. The genes are then inserted into viruses and given to patients through an injection. These genes then prompt cells to create antibodies. Although it's a different technique, the effect is the same as a vaccination—it would prevent infection. Human trials testing I.G.T. are likely to begin soon.

FIGHTING
EBOLA

In December 2013, a two-year-old boy in the West African nation of Guinea came down with a mysterious illness. He had a fever, black feces, and was vomiting. Only days later, he was dead. Cases of the disease continued showing up. In March 2014, Guinea's Ministry of Health sent samples of the virus to the Institut Pasteur in Paris, France. The tests came back. It was the Ebola virus in one of its deadliest forms. Ebola first appeared in 1976 and has periodically cropped up in West Africa. Vomiting, fever, and diarrhea can be followed by internal bleeding and death.

Within weeks, the virus was detected in Liberia. Two months later it appeared in Sierra Leone. The first case was diagnosed in Nigeria in July. The United Nations health agency soon declared an international public health emergency. Since that time, more than 11,000 people have died from the disease, many times the number of deaths from all other Ebola outbreaks combined.[8]

Vaccine testing was ongoing as the Ebola crisis continued in 2015. Two vaccines, ChAd3-ZEBOV and VSV-EBOV, had passed initial safety tests in humans and were in clinical trials to assess their effectiveness. Additional vaccines are in early test phases. In July 2015, a study from the Galveston National Laboratory in Texas had promising results in primates for an inhalable vaccine. An inhalable vaccine would be an advantage over an injected one because it wouldn't need trained health-care workers to administer it. The hope is that new technologies to prevent and treat the disease will help to fight off future outbreaks.

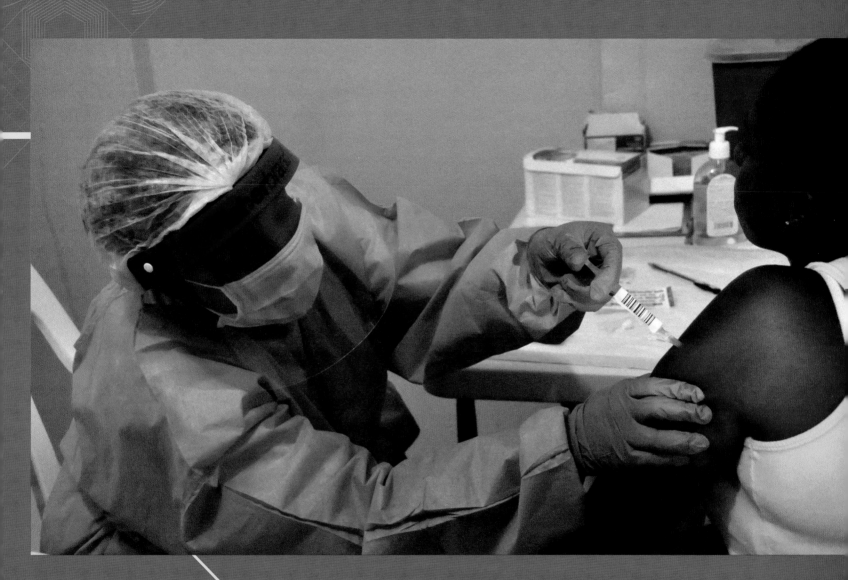

A woman participates in a clinical trial for an Ebola vaccine.

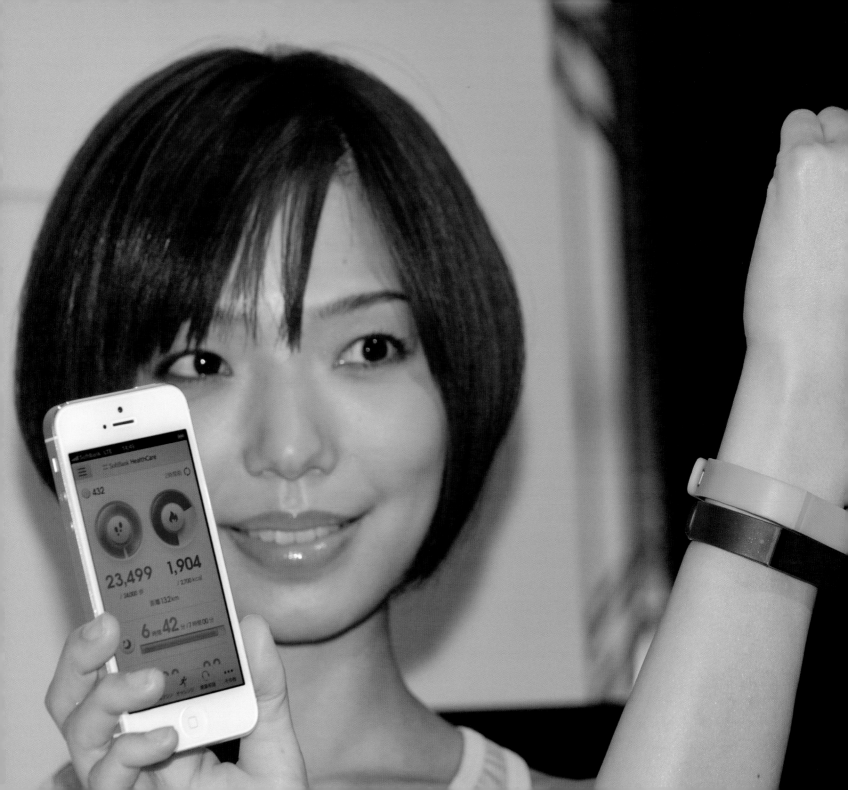

SEVEN

DATA-DRIVEN
HEALTH CARE

The number of people tracking their health through mobile devices has surged in recent years, prompting companies from Apple to Nike to Google to develop apps and online platforms that help patients collect and share their data with health professionals. A recent study shows a majority of adults in the United States track a health indicator for themselves or a loved one. Sixty percent of US adults track their weight, diet, or exercise routine, while one-third of adults track health indicators such as blood pressure, headaches, or sleep patterns. Twenty-one percent of people who track their health use technology, such as a smartphone, to do it.[1]

People with chronic conditions, such as diabetes, obesity, high blood pressure, and heart disease, are reportedly more likely to track their health, according to a national survey. And since the number of Americans living with a chronic illness is projected to reach 157 million by 2020, the market for mobile apps to track these diseases is

A variety of wristband fitness trackers communicate directly with users' smartphones.

growing daily.[2] If patients can track their own health measures and have that information automatically sent to their health-care providers, unnecessary trips to the doctor's office can be avoided. A 2008 analysis conducted by Brookings Institution economist Robert Litan found that, in the United States, tracking devices could save as much as $197 billion over the next 25 years.[3]

Tracking Apps

Smartphone apps send alerts for high or low blood sugar levels and allow diabetes patients to track insulin doses. Some apps allow patients to hold their phones against their chests to record their heart rate. Then the app sends the data to their doctors. Other apps provide medication reminders, record symptoms, or help schedule doctor visits. There are even apps that help patients track their sleep, their mood, or the number of steps they take each day. Health tracking gives patients more control over monitoring medical conditions and can provide doctors with more comprehensive data to help them choose treatment options.

In 2014, the Minnesota-based Mayo Clinic reported the results of a heart-health rehabilitation program that tested the effects of a smartphone-based app used to track health. The study included

A patient and doctor demonstrate a blood pressure device that sends results to any computer.

patients who were hospitalized following a heart attack. When they returned home, half of the patient group was given an app to record health metrics, such as weight, blood pressure, diet, and exercise. The app then provided advice on how to stay healthy and

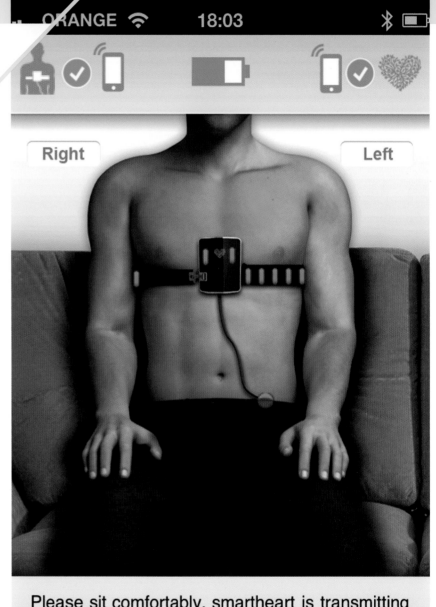

A smartphone can monitor a person's heart rate by measuring its electric activity and report the results via an app.

avoid further heart problems. Among patients who used the app, only 20 percent were readmitted to the hospital within 90 days of discharge, compared to 60 percent of those who didn't use the app.[6] The Mayo Clinic has since partnered with Apple on its new health app and data-sharing system.

Self-tracking devices are also being used to provide access to medical care in remote areas where clinics and hospitals are limited or nonexistent. In Japan, for example, some rural communities have been given wireless devices that record blood pressure, weight, and distance walked. This information is sent to distant doctors, who then make recommendations based on the data.

Tracking Mental Health

Researchers are still seeking ways to use technology to track one of the most widespread chronic health conditions: mental illness. Nearly 20 percent of US

A "Worried Well" Generation

In April 2015, UK-based general practitioner Des Spence published an article in the medical journal *BMJ*. He asserted that self-tracking apps and devices are creating an overly anxious population with no real symptoms. He calls this a "worried well" generation. Spence said the tracking apps are "untested and unscientific" and they will ultimately lead to extreme anxiety in people who are otherwise healthy. Spence claims the groups that stand to benefit most from the obsession with tracking devices and over-monitored personal health care are the drug industry and corporate medicine. "Witness the . . . bogus screening and exponential growth of invented non-diseases," he wrote.[8] Users should not expect these apps to provide accurate medical diagnoses, Spence argues. Rather, diagnoses should be left to trained physicians who can interpret results.

adults suffer from a mental illness, according to the National Institute of Mental Health.[7] But the nature of mental illnesses such as depression, bipolar disorder, schizophrenia, anxiety, and post-traumatic stress disorder (PTSD) is such that symptoms are not easy to measure with simple tracking devices. Some apps track mood or behavior through surveys the patients fill out. Others send reminders about taking medications. But the options are limited.

Researchers at the University of Maryland are trying to overcome those challenges. They are developing an app to record various markers—heart rate, skin temperature, voice, facial expressions, and language—that could help track mental health. Other companies such as Ginger.io and Mobilyze record things such as an increase in missed calls or texts, changes in sleep cycles (recorded through sleep sensors), or changes in movement (recorded through Global Positioning System [GPS] sensors). This data is combined with information users supply about their mood and social context. When risk factors are present, the app sends the user advice on taking action to prevent depression. It can also connect the user to a health-care provider.

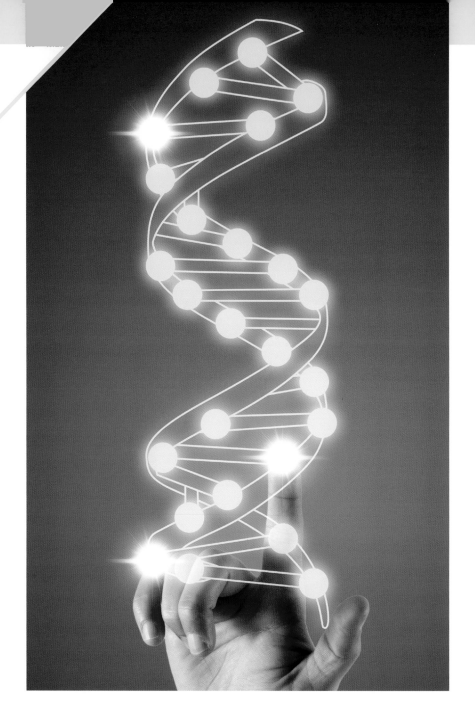

Your DNA can reveal a lot about you and your health.

The Challenges

There are some concerns about the privacy and regulatory issues that come with digital tracking and data sharing. Technology can help people to assess risk factors, signs, and symptoms of diseases, which helps doctors diagnose conditions. Through self-tracking and genetic testing, methods to assess and monitor health risks are increasingly inexpensive and accessible. But there are major concerns with patient privacy. Some health tracking technologies, such as measuring your steps or calorie intake, appear relatively harmless. But there are other cases where accidentally shared information could be harmful to the patient, such as with a diagnosis of cancer or a chronic syndrome.

One major concern is the potential for insurance companies or employers to discriminate based on an individual's genetic profile. Congress addressed this issue in 2008 with the Genetic Information Nondiscrimination Act. This law "protects Americans from being treated unfairly because of differences in their DNA that may affect their health."[9]

Another issue is who owns the data. Standard confidentiality agreements apply if the data is being used by a physician. But if the data is being collected by a company that is helping track it, the privacy rules are much hazier. In many cases, they are nonexistent.

Beyond insurance or privacy concerns, there are psychological effects to knowing about a risk for a disease years before any signs or symptoms will present themselves. Some people may find the knowledge empowering, while it may worry others.

Regulations are needed to manage the quality of the thousands of health apps available. But too many regulations may stifle innovation in the technology industry. Policy makers are struggling to find the right balance that protects consumers while encouraging new discoveries.

◢ A Privacy Slip

Fitbit is a San Francisco-based company that makes wristband tracking devices that monitor activity levels, exercise, food intake, weight, and sleep, while also providing progress reports on fitness goals. Users also have the options of tracking sexual activity. According to Fitbit's current website, its privacy policy is clear: "Your fitness journey is your own. You should be able to share what you want, when you want. That's why we don't sell your private data—and why we never budge on privacy."[11] But Fitbit hasn't always been diligent about privacy settings. In 2011, the sexual activity records of 200 Fitbit users showed up in Google search results.[12] Once the company was notified of the privacy breach, it swiftly hid all user activity records and requested that search engines delete the data. But the event left many wondering how secure their data is.

In January 2015, the FDA indicated it will only be lightly regulating what it terms "low risk general wellness" products, such as apps that track the number of steps you take each day or your total caloric intake.[10] If the intended use of a product is to diagnose or treat a specific disease, or if it presents a

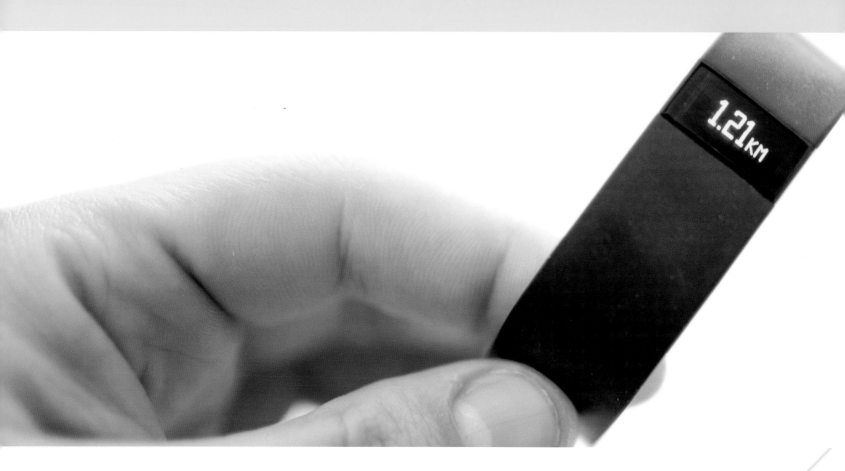

Self-tracking helps many achieve health goals, but it can contribute to unhealthy behavior such as helping people with anorexia eat too little.

safety risk, a more rigorous review would be required. Some experts agree with this position, arguing that a minimal review process helps promote innovation in a rapidly growing field. Others, however, worry the FDA's approach encourages the development of untested, and therefore unscientific, products. Some products market themselves as medical apps but include disclaimers that release them from blame if the diagnosis is wrong.

Untested or faulty products have already hit the market, only to be recalled. In 2011, for example, Pfizer warned doctors its Rheumatology Calculator app was giving the wrong scores for measuring tender and swollen joints in arthritis patients and requested that doctors delete the app. A year later, Sanofi Aventis recalled a diabetes app that was giving the wrong insulin doses.

Proponents of the self-tracking movement say that millions of people track themselves all the time, whether it's recording weight, noting exercise, or counting calories. The difference today is how that information is recorded. Unlike simple pen and paper, keeping records through digital and mobile devices allows for quicker and more meaningful analysis. When this is combined with the ability to send information directly to a health-care provider, self-tracking has the potential to be extremely useful.

◢23andMe

In 2007, a new company called 23andMe offered consumers access to their genetic data through a simple saliva test. For $99, customers received ancestry information and a variety of health reports based on their genetic data, such as a patient's risk of developing breast cancer and what their potential response to treatment might be. In 2013, the FDA issued a warning letter to 23andMe, declaring that marketing the genome service kit was in violation of the Federal Food, Drug and Cosmetic Act. It crossed the line between a "low risk general wellness" product, which does not require regulatory approval, and a diagnostic and treatment service, which does. But in February 2015, the FDA shifted its stance, allowing 23andMe to market a genetic test for Bloom Syndrome, an inherited disorder that causes short stature and leads to an increased risk of cancer.

EIGHT

THE LAUNCH OF
TELEMEDICINE

The term *telemedicine* was coined in the 1970s. It refers to the use of information and communication technologies to provide patient care. The earliest adoption of modern telemedicine occurred in the 1960s by the National Aeronautics and Space Administration (NASA). Physicians measured astronauts' heart rate, blood pressure, breathing, and temperature to better understand the effects of lower gravity on humans. It wasn't long before telemedicine transitioned from space consultations to Earth.

Telemedicine has played a particularly important role in improving access to medical services in remote regions where health-care options are limited. And with an increasingly limited number of doctors around the world, telemedicine has the potential to provide medical services to patients where they otherwise wouldn't exist.

Using videoconferencing, doctors can see patients long-distance.

81

There will be a shortage of 45,000 primary care physicians and 46,000 surgeons and medical specialists in the United States by the year 2020. Getting access to medical care in rural areas, where roughly 20 percent of the population lives, is a major challenge.[1] For example, there are only three intensive care centers for children in Oregon. All three are based in Portland. Telemedicine in the form of videoconferencing allows doctors in rural areas to consult with pediatricians about critical cases.

Massachusetts General Hospital launched a TeleHealth initiative in 2012. One aspect of this program includes telemedicine sessions for burn victims. Patients in a rehabilitation hospital wishing to see a burn specialist at Mass General must travel via ambulance, which can be uncomfortable for people recovering from burns. It also forces them to lose valuable rehabilitation time. Telemedicine allows patients to connect directly with their specialist on a regular basis with little inconvenience or pain. One patient, a survivor of the Boston Marathon bombing in 2013, connected with his burn specialist through a video conference, which allowed him to show the doctor his wounds and range of motion without having to leave his rehabilitation facility.

A robot with a video screen allows remote doctors to make the rounds at a hospital.

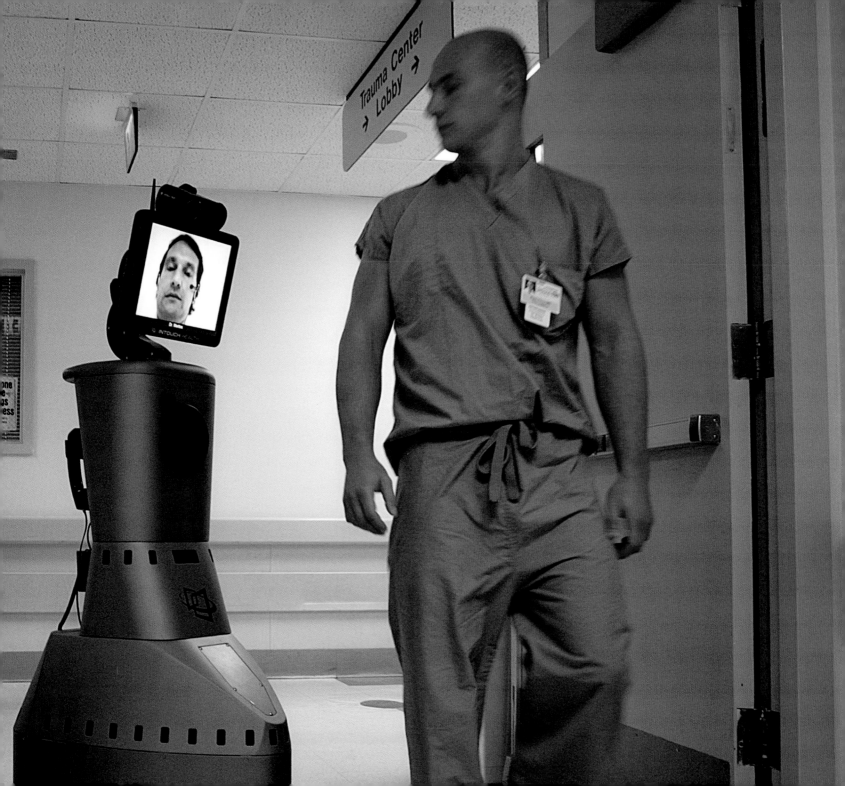

Therapy on Your Own Couch

Cognitive behavioral therapy (CBT) is an approach to therapy that aims to change patterns of thinking or behavior. In 2009, researchers tested the effect of CBT delivered online by a therapist for patients with depression. Patients were separated into two groups. One group received normal care from their general practitioner. The other group received online CBT in addition to usual care. The researchers found that after four months the group that received the online CBT was more likely to recover from depression than patients in the group that did not. Online therapy has the potential to increase access to mental health care.

Telemedicine is often mentioned as a way to improve the management of chronic diseases by empowering patients to track their health and reduce the need for unnecessary follow-up visits. A 2014 study looked at using telemedicine to manage three chronic conditions: congestive heart failure, stroke, and chronic obstructive pulmonary disease. The researchers found considerable evidence that telemedicine is an effective method of treating these conditions. Hospital admissions were reduced, as were the number of days patients stayed in the hospital. Unnecessary emergency room visits were avoided. The researchers also found using telemedicine helped to prevent illnesses, thereby improving the overall health of patients.

A school nurse in rural Texas conducts an exam while a doctor from Houston consults via videoconference.

One of the primary users of telemedicine services are working parents, according to the CEO of Doctor on Demand, a telemedicine provider. Through the Doctor on Demand program, caregivers can access one of more than 1,000 doctors through their smartphones and receive a diagnosis and a treatment plan via video. This helps people whose schedules are too busy to take time off work and plan a trip to the doctor's office.

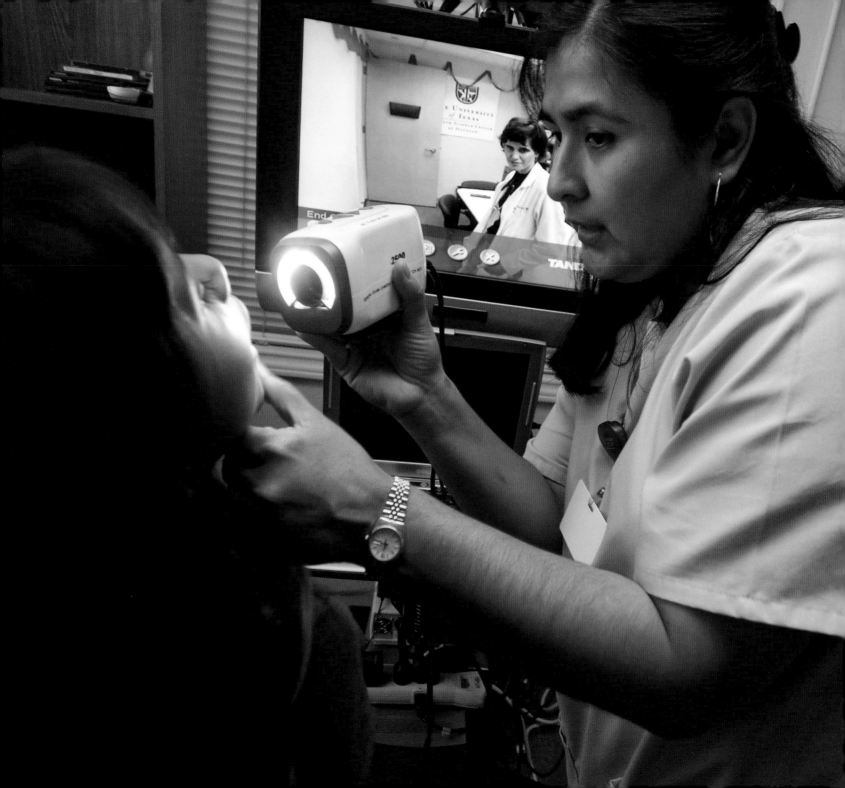

New technology, such as the portable ultrasound machine, helps medical workers in rural areas lacking facilities, equipment, or reliable electricity.

Mobile Telemedicine around the World

Other doctors are testing strategies using mobile devices to support patient care. This type of telemedicine is often referred to as mobile health, or mHealth. This strategy is especially welcome in remote areas where there are few doctors and little equipment. One company developed software that enabled health workers in Malawi to text medical information about routine symptoms of their rural patients to health clinics in more urban areas. The health workers would then receive a quick diagnosis and suggested treatments. Within the first six months after the project launched the number of patients treated for tuberculosis doubled, more than 1,200 hours in travel time were saved, and new emergency services became available in the area. The cost of running the system for six months was just $500.[2]

Doctors in rural areas of China have mobile devices that can retrieve electronic medical records and offer access to databases that provide additional background information on medical conditions. For more complicated medical conditions, doctors in these communities use the mobile devices to communicate with health providers in urban centers.

The Red Tape

The response to telemedicine has been mixed. Some doctors and patients are reluctant to change the dynamic of the in-person doctor/patient interaction. Others aren't well-versed in the technology and are unable to use it effectively.

Critics of telemedicine are not only concerned about losing out on the doctor/patient relationship that develops during in-person visits. They also worry telemedicine may not offer the same quality of care. One study looked at the difference between e-visits—where patients enter their symptoms and information in an online portal and the medical worker offers a diagnosis and treatment through the same portal—and face-to-face visits. The aim was to compare the accuracy of the diagnoses, how follow-up visits are scheduled, and whether antibiotic drugs are overprescribed. The researchers found the follow-up visit rate was about the same, but doctors were much more likely to prescribe antibiotics during e-visits than face-to-face.

Telemedicine has faced significant challenges. One major barrier to adopting telemedicine is state regulations, which can limit or ban the practice of telemedicine. While most states are increasing access to telemedicine services due to doctor shortages, some are slow to expand services over concerns about patient safety.

Telemedicine is becoming more widely practiced and accepted today, but some doctors remain concerned over potential liability issues, patient safety, or changes in the way physicians practice medicine. Patient privacy is also a concern—can self-tracking combined with telemedicine approaches to health care be properly secured? Despite the concerns, given the issue of doctor shortages, telemedicine may be the only option in some areas.

Some worry the doctor-patient relationship is impaired when telemedicine is substituted for in-person visits.

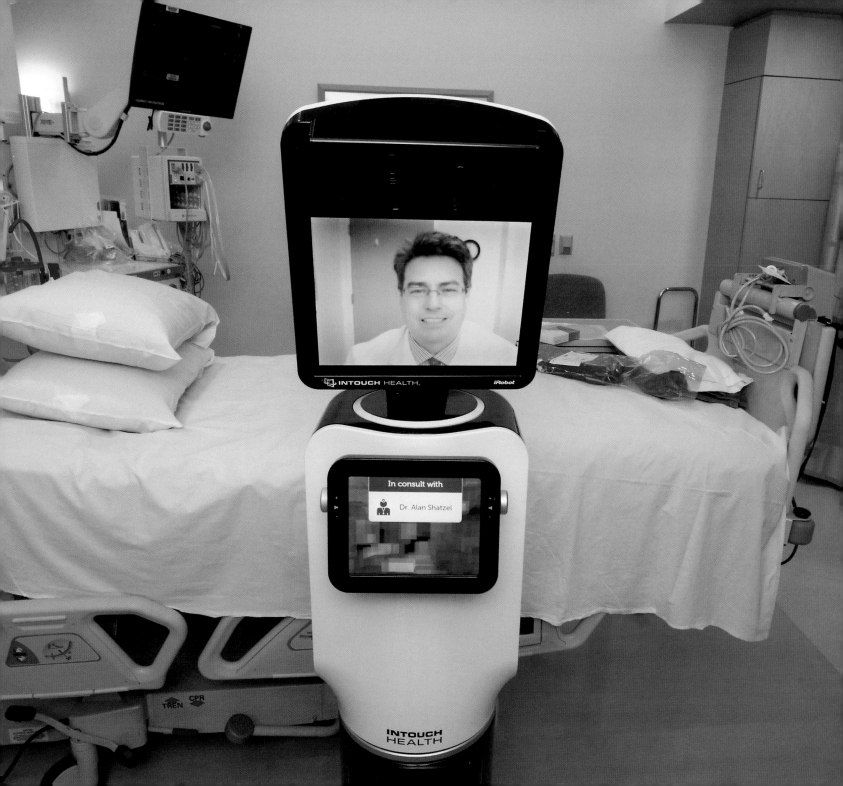

In consult with

Dr. Alan Shatzel

INTOUCH HEALTH

INTOUCH HEALTH.   iRobot

NINE

ROBOTS AND SUPERCOMPUTERS ARE COMING!

In science fiction, the word *robot* typically conjures up images of human-shaped machines that mimic human movements and respond to commands. But there are a variety of supercomputers and robots today that are being used in the field of medicine. Supercomputers can process a wealth of medical literature and patient history in seconds to arrive at an evidence-based diagnosis. Robots can improve surgical procedures by making them less invasive, manage charts and vital signs, and patrol patient hallways on rounds. Scientists even imagine a future in which microscopic robots enter the human body and deliver drugs or repair damage.

Preparing for a shortage of nurses in the coming decades, researchers in Japan are working on helper robots that can lift patients in and out of beds.

IBM's Watson

Watson, a supercomputer developed by IBM, was built to mimic the same learning process as humans use: observe, interpret, evaluate, and decide. Watson gained its star status in 2011 after it defeated its human competitors on the television quiz show *Jeopardy!*, marking a significant advance in the field of artificial intelligence, or thinking machines. Watson proved it is capable of retaining large quantities of data, as well as understanding language, coming up with hypotheses based on evidence, and actively learning. But researchers at IBM had bigger plans for the supercomputer that extended far beyond a game show. They saw enormous potential in the health-care industry, where Watson could be used to support medical decision-making.

Watson is now working with hospitals around the country, including Memorial Sloan Kettering Cancer Center, Mayo Clinic, the New York Genome Center, Cleveland Clinic, and the University of Texas MD Anderson Cancer Center. IBM executives designed Watson to help gather and organize the massive amount of data that is being collected through self-tracking devices and other technologies to help health-care providers make better, more informed decisions.

Watson has limitless applications. An Internet-connected toy dinosaur links to Watson so it can answer children's questions in natural language.

Watson for Oncology

At Memorial Sloan Kettering Cancer Center in New York, clinicians and analysts have partnered with IBM to train Watson to interpret a patient's clinical information. The aim is to help doctors arrive at a treatment option that is based on a massive amount of data, more than any one physician could hope to analyze. Initially, researchers trained Watson to focus on patient data related to breast and lung cancers, but they have since included more than a dozen other cancers. The computer is being trained to interpret physician notes, lab results, and clinical research, as well as a patient's medical history, medications, which cancer therapy he or she received, and what their response was.

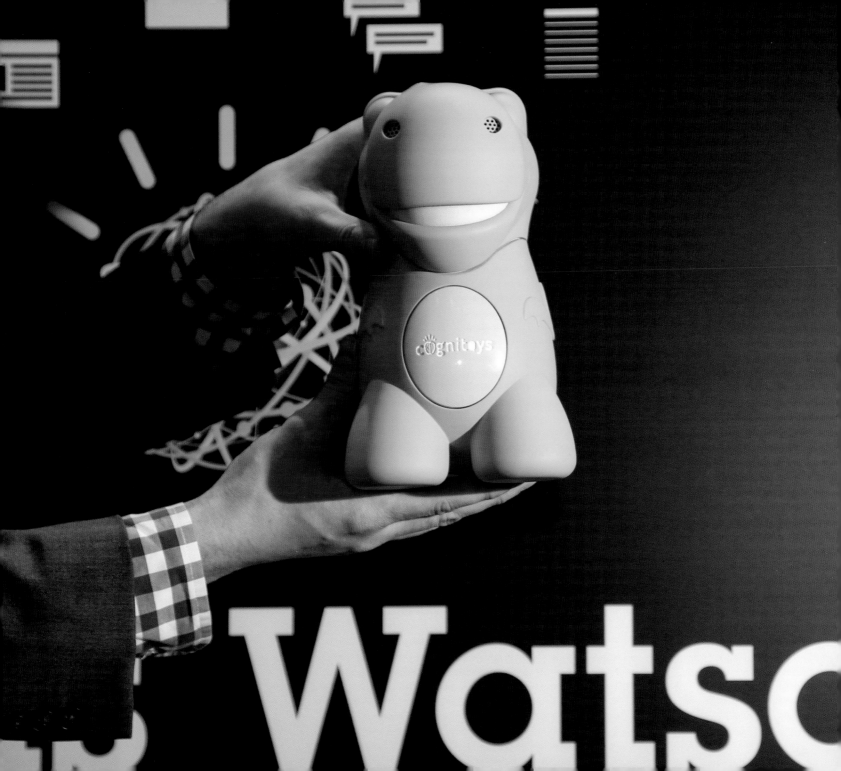

The analysis happens in a matter of seconds, and the computer translates this information into treatment recommendations for an individual patient's cancer.

Given the wealth of information Watson is able to retain, the supercomputer is well equipped to rapidly identify patients for clinical trials that test new and emerging drugs to treat a given condition. In the fall of 2014, IBM and the Mayo Clinic announced a partnership to launch a new program in which Watson matches cancer patients with appropriate clinical trials, a task that takes clinical coordinators a considerable amount of time to accomplish. With Watson, patients are allowed access to potential treatments almost immediately. Watson is also able to help find patients who have rare diseases and might qualify for a drug trial.

Surgical Robots

In 2000, the California-based company Intuitive Surgical received FDA approval to allow surgeons to use its da Vinci robotic system to assist with minimally invasive surgeries, such as those that involve sending tiny cameras and tools into the body through small incisions, and other medical procedures. Da Vinci, named after artist Leonardo da Vinci, who designed the first robot in 1495, has been used in more than 1.5 million procedures since its approval.[1]

An Austrian man shows off his bionic hand, among the first in the world that is controlled by the user's thoughts.

The system has four arms used to control instruments that can open and close incisions and perform other tasks. The surgeon controls the instruments while looking into a display generated by a three-dimensional high-definition camera. The aim of using the robot is to enable greater vision, precision, and control.

Although robotic surgery has generated a great deal of excitement for both the patient and the surgeon, some argue it's unclear whether the method actually improves patient care. One thing that is clear, however, is its potential to provide medical services to patients in remote areas that don't have

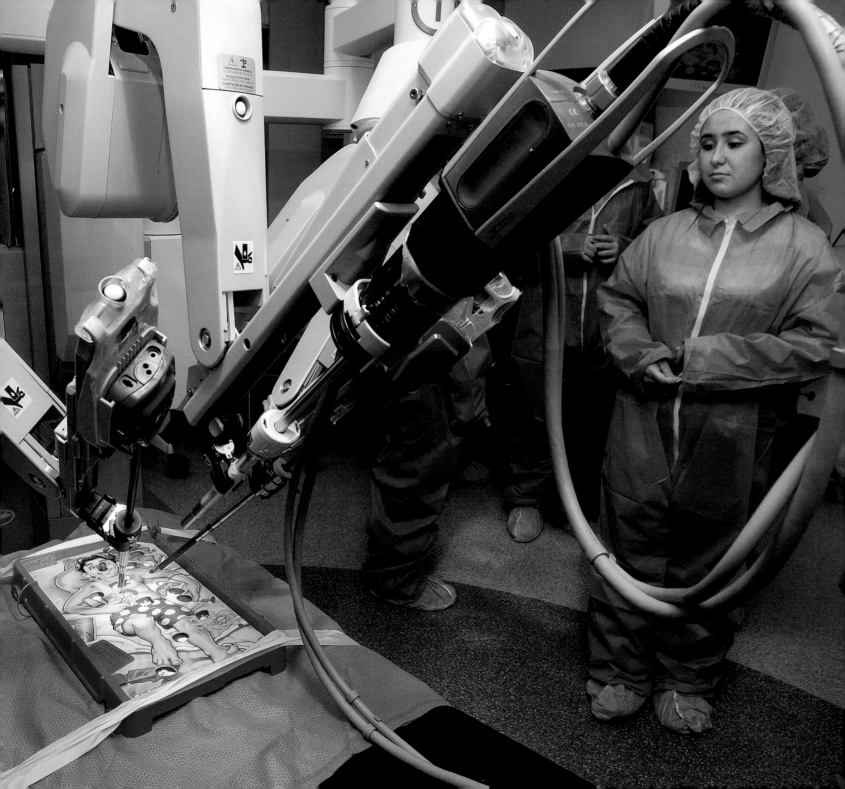

High school robotics students get a chance to practice running a da Vinci system, using it to play the board game Operation.

access to physicians who can perform these procedures. In some cases, and in places where there are few doctors, it is more cost effective to equip a health facility with a robot than to have a surgeon in-house—allowing the health facility to share a surgeon with other institutions. Surgeons can use surgery robots to perform operations without being in the same place as the patient, a procedure known as telesurgery. Doctors can look into and move the robotic camera while directing nurses who are present in the room with the patient.

In March 2015, Google partnered with medical device and drug company Johnson and Johnson to improve the technology of surgical robots by using artificial intelligence. The idea is to take a da Vinci-style robot to the next level. This would not only enable surgeons to perform minimally invasive surgery from a control station, but it would also provide information to help guide the surgeon's decision-making. Although Google has not released its own official information about this partnership, an article published in *Wired* quoted the company as saying that a new system would "help surgeons see better during surgery or help them more easily access information they rely on as they operate." The same article said a Johnson and Johnson spokesperson referred to it as the "Google Maps for surgery."[2]

An Octopus Inspires a Flexible Robot

Octopuses are famous for their ability to squeeze into tiny spaces by softening their bodies and sliding around obstacles. They can also stiffen their tentacles to catch prey. An elephant trunk works in a similar way. Inspired by the unique abilities of these animals, a European company called STIFF-FLOP (STIFFness controllable Flexible and Learn-able Manipulator for surgical OPerations) is developing a robotic arm that can soften and harden on command. The robot would be a huge asset in minimally invasive surgeries. Unlike standard surgical instruments that must move in a straight line, STIFF-FLOP would be capable of sliding around soft organs without damaging them.

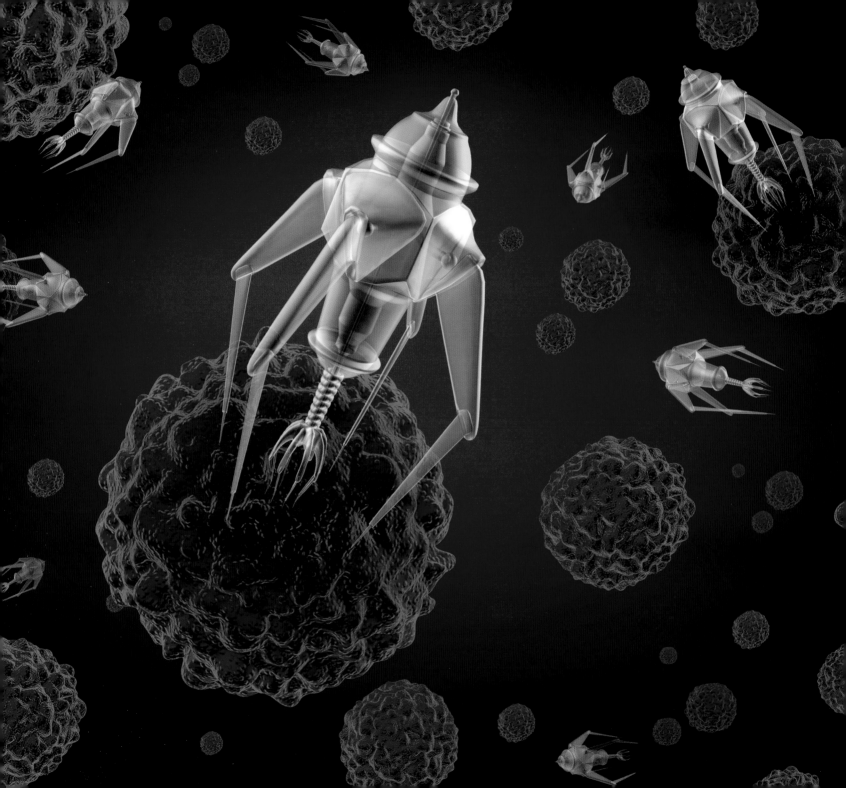

In the future, scientists hope to develop microscopic robots that will fight disease inside the human body.

As some robots become larger and more powerful, others are shrinking in size. In the future, scientists hope to create microscopic nanorobots that will enter the human body to precisely deliver tiny doses of medicine or use microtools such as lasers to zap cancer cells or clean out unhealthy buildup in cells. Microbots 0.04 inches (1 mm) around have been developed, but they must shrink much smaller to be able to target cancer cells, infections, and other damage from the inside.

From robots performing surgery, to printing and transplanting entire human organs, to harnessing a patient's own immune system to fight cancer, technology is advancing the field of medicine at an unprecedented rate. But with these advances comes a host of ethical challenges. How do we protect and secure patient data? How do we prevent potentially fatal errors? Nevertheless, cutting-edge research advances have helped find answers to what were once unsolvable medical mysteries.

◢ Robots Face Security Threats

As the role of medical and surgical robots expands, scientists have begun asking themselves what would happen if the computer systems that power these machines were hacked. Could the robots be turned into weapons? A group of researchers from the University of Washington began to investigate by testing a variety of cybersecurity threats on Raven II, a teleoperated surgical robot system. They found they were able to hack into the system, manipulate the robot, and override the surgeon's command inputs. Surgical and other medical robots used in today's hospitals and health facilities rely on secure networks. But these threats are particularly relevant when it comes to implementing these robotic procedures in remote settings, where secure networks may not exist.

ESSENTIAL FACTS

Key Discoveries

» **Gene therapy:** This experimental technique uses a patient's genes to treat or prevent disease. The method has been successful in treating certain cancer patients, and it is now being tested on other diseases, including HIV, malaria, influenza, and hepatitis.

» **Immunotherapy:** Immunotherapy harnesses the immune system to fight cancer. Recent advances in this cancer treatment method have pushed it to the top of the list of recent medical breakthroughs.

» **Three-dimensional printed organs:** New methods to generate human organs in the lab using a patient's own cells may help lessen the organ donation shortage in the United States. Advances in technology have helped scientists get closer to 3-D printing human kidneys—one of the most challenging organs to develop, but one with the greatest potential for saving lives.

Key Players

» **Anthony Atala:** Atala developed a technique for growing transplantable organs using a patient's own cells to avoid organ rejection.

» **Doug Melton:** Melton and his team took a big step toward curing type 1 diabetes by creating insulin-producing beta cells from stem cells.

» **George Church:** Church spearheaded the Personal Genome Project, which shares human genetic information with researchers around the world.

» **James Allison:** Allison pioneered the use of immunotherapy to fight cancer.

Key Tools and Technologies

» **Robots:** Increasingly smart and versatile robots are allowing doctors to better diagnose illness, perform safer surgeries, and see patients remotely.

» **Self-tracking devices:** Self-tracking devices allow patients to keep track of vital statistics, helping them take their health care into their own hands.

» **Three-dimensional printing:** Three-dimensional printing allows scientists to create organs in the lab.

Future Outlook

Technological innovations in health care have revolutionized the field. Emerging health threats and challenges, from infectious diseases to chronic health conditions, are being met with medical advances and a focus on treating individual patients.

Quote

"This surgery came along and basically made me who I am today and saved my life."

—*Luke Massella, one of the first patients to receive a bladder generated from his own cells*

GLOSSARY

antibody

A protein produced by the body in response to a foreign antigen such as a bacterium or toxin.

antigen

A foreign substance or microorganism that stimulates the immune system to produce antibodies when it enters the body.

biomaterial

A type of material that is created in a lab and can be implanted in the body.

chemotherapy

A cancer treatment that uses chemicals.

cloud

A network of remote, Internet-hosted servers that manage and process data.

DNA

A substance, deoxyribonucleic acid, that exists in the cells of plants and animals and carries genetic material.

enzyme

A chemical substance in plants and animals that helps cause natural processes such as digestion.

gene

The part of a DNA molecule that transmits hereditary information and directs cell operations.

genome

An organism's complete set of DNA.

inflammation

Swelling.

mammography

The X-ray examination of breasts to detect cancer.

metastatic

A cancer that has spread to other parts of the body.

prodrug

A drug that is inactive until it gets inside a patient's body.

ADDITIONAL RESOURCES

Selected Bibliography

American Association for the Advancement of Science. "Breakthroughs of the Year." *Science*. 19 Dec. 2014: 1444–1449. Print and web.

"Cancer Facts and Figures 2015." *American Cancer Society*. American Cancer Society, 2015. Web. 16 May 2015.

Fox, Susannah, and Maeve Duggan. "Tracking for Health." *Pew Research Center*. Pew Research Center, 28 Jan. 2013. Web. 16 May 2015.

"Vaccines." *National Institute of Allergy and Infectious Diseases*. National Institute of Allergy and Infectious Diseases, 19 Apr. 2011. Web. 16 May 2015.

Zimmer, Carl. "Protection without a Vaccine." *New York Times*. New York Times, 9 Mar. 2015. Web. 16 May 2015.

Further Readings

Carmichael, L. E. *Gene Therapy*. Minneapolis, MN: Abdo, 2014.

Schafer, Susan. *Heredity*. Armonk, NY: M. E. Sharp, 2009.

Websites

To learn more about Cutting-Edge Science and Technology, visit **booklinks.abdopublishing.com**. These links are routinely monitored and updated to provide the most current information available.

For More Information

For more information on this subject, contact or visit the following organizations:

Centers for Disease Control and Prevention

1600 Clifton Road
Atlanta, GA 30329-4027 USA
800-CDC-INFO
http://cdc.gov

The CDC is a United States federal agency that operates under the Department of Health and Human Services. It is the leading national public health institute in the United States working to study and prevent disease, injury, and disability.

Mayo Clinic

200 First Street Southwest
Rochester, MN 55905
507-284-2511
http://mayoclinic.org

Mayo Clinic is a nonprofit medical care, research, and education institute, and was recognized as the best hospital in the nation for 2014–2015. Mayo Clinic is based in Rochester, Minnesota, although it has locations in many other states.

SOURCE NOTES

Chapter 1. Growing New Organs

1. "Organ Procurement and Transplantation Network." *US Department of Health and Human Services*. US Department of Health and Human Services, 27 July 2015. Web. 27 July 2015.

2. "Anthony Atala: Printing a Human Kidney." *TED*. TED, Mar. 2011. Web. 27 July 2015.

3. "Organ Procurement and Transplantation Network: Data." *US Department of Health and Human Services*. US Department of Health and Human Services, 27 July 2015. Web. 27 July 2015.

4. "Life Expectancy." *Centers for Disease Control*. CDC, 29 Apr. 2015. Web. 27 July 2015.

Chapter 2. Fighting Cancer with the Immune System

1. Jennifer Couzin-Frankel. "Cancer Immunotherapy." *Science* 342 (2013): 1432–1433. Web. 27 July 2015.

2. Marcia McNutt. "Cancer Immunotherapy." *Science* 342 (2013): 1417. Web. 27 July 2015.

3. Jason Kane. "If Cancer's Not a War, What Is It?" *PBS Newshour*. Newshour Productions, 23 Dec. 2011. Web. 27 July 2015.

4. Claudia Dreifus. "Arming the Immune System Against Cancer." *New York Times*. New York Times, 2 Mar. 2015. Web. 27 July 2015.

5. "Cancer Facts and Figures 2015." *American Cancer Society*. American Cancer Society, 2015. Web. 27 July 2015.

6. Jennifer Couzin-Frankel. "Cancer Immunotherapy." *Science* 342 (2013): 1432–1433. Web. 27 July 2015.

Chapter 3. Zeroing In on Cancer Cells

1. "Chemo Side Effects." *American Cancer Society*. American Cancer Society, 9 June 2015. Web. 27 July 2015.

2. Andrew M. Scott, James P. Allison, and Jedd D. Wolchok. "Monoclonal Antibodies in Cancer Therapy." *Cancer Immunity* 12 (1 May 2012). Web. 27 July 2015.

3. Ibid.

4. Katrin P. Guillen, Carla Kurkjian, and Roger G. Harrison. "Targeted Enzyme Prodrug Therapy for Metastatic Prostate Cancer—A Comparative Study of L-methioninase, Purine Nucleoside Phosphorylase, and Cytosine Deaminase," *Journal of Biomedical Science* 21 (July 2014). Web. 27 July 2015.

5. "SMDC Technology." *Endocyte*. Endocyte, 2014. Web. 27 July 2015.

Chapter 4. Genetics and Personalized Medicine

1. "FACT SHEET: President Obama's Precision Medicine Initiative." *The White House*. The White House, 30 Jan. 2015. Web. 27 July 2015.

2. Robert Pear. "US to Collect Genetic Data to Hone Care." *New York Times*. New York Times, 30 Jan. 2015. Web. 27 July 2015.

3. Brenda J. Wilson and Stuart G. Nicholls. "The Human Genome Project, and Recent Advances in Personalized Genomics." *Journal of Risk Management and Healthcare Policy* 8 (2015): 9–20. *National Center for Biotechnology Information, US National Library of Medicine*. Web. 27 July 2015.

4. Beverly Mertz. "Precision Medicine Is Coming, but Not Anytime Soon." *Harvard Health Publications*. Harvard Medical School, 26 Mar. 2015. Web. 27 July 2015.

5. The White House Office of the Press Secretary. "Remarks Made by the President, et al." *National Human Genome Research Institute*. NIH, 26 June 2000. Web. 27 July 2015.

6. "Hepatitis C FAQs for Health Professionals." *Centers for Disease Control and Prevention*. CDC, 31 May 2015. Web. 27 July 2015.

7. Angelina Jolie. "My Medical Choice." *New York Times*. New York Times, 14 May 2013. Web. 27 July 2015.

8. "An Expanded Timeline of Personalized Medicine." *Harvard Medicine*. Harvard Medical School, 2015. Web. 27 July 2015.

9. Chris Morrison. "$1 Million Price Tag Set for Glybera Gene Therapy." *Bioentrepreneur Trade Secrets*. Nature, 3 Mar. 2015. Web. 27 July 2015.

10. "Public Profile—hu43860C." *Personal Genome Project*. Personal Genome Project, n.d. Web. 27 July 2015.

Chapter 5. Confronting a Chronic Health Crisis

1. "Chronic Diseases: The Leading Causes of Death and Disability in the United States." *Centers for Disease Control and Prevention*. CDC, 18 May 2015. Web. 27 July 2015.

2. "What Are the Key Statistics about Breast Cancer?" *American Cancer Society*. American Cancer Society, 10 June 2015. Web. 27 July 2015.

3. S. M. Friedewald, et al. "Breast Cancer Screening Using Tomosynthesis in Combination with Digital Mammography." *JAMA* 311 (25 June 2014): 2499–2507. *National Center for Biotechnology Information, US National Library of Medicine*. Web. 27 July 2015.

4. "Diabetes Home: Data and Statistics." *Centers for Disease Control and Prevention*. CDC, 7 May 2015. Web. 27 July 2015.

5. Ibid.

6. "Diseases and Conditions: Type 1 Diabetes; Definition." *Mayo Clinic*. Mayo Clinic, 2 Aug. 2014. Web. 27 July 2015.

7. Ibid.

8. Grace Christ and Sadhna Diwan. "Chronic Illness and Aging." *Council on Social Work Education*. National Center for Gerontological Social Work Education, n.d. Web. 27 July 2015.

9. Jiaquan Xu, et al. "Mortality Data in the United States, 2012." *NCHS Data Brief* 168 (Oct. 2014). Web. *CDC*, 27 July 2015.

10. Grace Christ and Sadhna Diwan. "Chronic Illness and Aging." *Council on Social Work Education*. National Center for Gerontological Social Work Education, n.d. Web. 27 July 2015.

Chapter 6. Advances and Challenges in Vaccine Research

1. "Measles Cases and Outbreaks." *Centers for Disease Control and Prevention*. CDC, 30 June 2015. Web. 27 July 2015.

2. "Diseases and Conditions: Smallpox; Symptoms." *Mayo Clinic*. Mayo Clinic, 16 Aug. 2014. Web. 27 July 2015.

3. Walter A. Orenstein, et al. "Contemporary Vaccine Challenges: Improving Global Health One Shot at a Time." *Science Translational Medicine*. 6 (10 Sept. 2014). Web. 27 July 2015.

4. "HIV/AIDS: Pre-exposure Prophylaxis." *Centers for Disease Control and Prevention*. CDC, 25 June 2015. Web. 27 July 2015.

5. RTS,S Clinical Trials Partnership. "Efficacy and Safety of RTS,S/AS01 Malaria Vaccine with or without a Booster Dose in Infants and Children in Africa." *Lancet* 386 (July 2015): 31–45. Web. 27 July 2015.

6. Sarah Boseley. "Malaria Vaccine a Breakthrough despite Being Partially Effective, Say Scientists." *Guardian*. Guardian News and Media, 23 Apr. 2015. Web. 27 July 2015.

7. "Valeant Offers $296 Million for Dendreon's Prostate Cancer Drug Provenge." *FDA News Drug Daily Bulletin*. FDA News, 6 Feb. 2015. Web. 27 July 2015.

8. "2014 Ebola Outbreak in West Africa—Case Counts." *Centers for Disease Control and Prevention*. CDC, 24 July 2015. Web. 27 July 2015.

Chapter 7. Data-Driven Health Care

1. Susannah Fox and Maeve Duggan. "Tracking for Health." *Pew Research Center*. Pew Research Center, 28 Jan. 2013. Web. 27 July 2015.

2. Thomas Bodenheimer, Ellen Chen, and Heather D. Bennett. "Confronting the Growing Burden of Chronic Disease: Can the US Health Care Workforce Do the Job?" *Health Affairs* 28.1 (Jan./Feb. 2009): 64–74. Web. 27 July 2015.

3. Darrell West. "How Mobile Devices Are Transforming Healthcare." *Issues in Technology Innovation* 18 (May 2012). *Center for Technology Innovation at Brookings*. Web. 27 July 2015.

4. "Quantified Self Meetups." *Quantified Self Meetups*. Quantified Self, n.d. Web. 27 July 2015.

5. Gary Wolf. "The Data-Driven Life." *New York Times*. New York Times, 28 Apr. 2010. Web. 27 July 2015.

6. Traci Klein. "Mayo Research Shows Cardiac Rehab Patients Who Use Smartphone App Recover Better." *Mayo Clinic News Network*. Mayo Clinic, 29 Mar. 2014. Web. 27 July 2015.

7. "Any Mental Illness (AMI) Among Adults." *National Institute of Mental Health*. NIH, n.d. Web. 27 July 2015.

8. Iltifat Husain and Des Spence. "Head to Head: Can Healthy People Benefit from Health Apps?" *BMJ* 350 (Apr. 2015): 1–3. Web. 27 July 2015.

9. "Genetic Information Nondiscrimination Act of 2008." *National Human Genome Research Institute*. NIH, 6 Apr. 2015. Web. 27 July 2015.

10. "General Wellness: Policy for Low Risk Devices. Draft Guidance for Industry and Food and Drug Administration Staff." *US Food and Drug Administration: Center for Devices and Radiological Health*. US Department of Health and Human Services, 20 Jan. 2015. Web. 27 July 2015.

11. "Why Fitbit?" *Fitbit*. Fitbit, n.d. Web. 27 July 2015.

12. Kashmir Hill. "Fitbit Moves Quickly after Users' Sex Stats Exposed." *Forbes*. Forbes, 5 Nov. 2014. Web. 27 July 2015.

Chapter 8. The Launch of Telemedicine

1. "Physician Shortages to Worsen Without Increases in Residency Training." *Association of American Medical Colleges*. AAMC, n.d. Web. 27 July 2015.

2. Chris Sweeney. "How Text Messages Could Change Global Healthcare." *Popular Mechanics*. Hearst Communications, 24 Oct. 2011. Web. 27 July 2015.

Chapter 9. Robots and Supercomputers Are Coming!

1. "Da Vinci Surgery: Frequently Asked Questions." *Intuitive Surgical*. Intuitive Surgical, 2015. Web. 27 July 2015.

2. Tim Moynihan. "Google Takes on the Challenge of Making Robot Surgery Safer." *Wired*. Condé Nast, 30 Mar. 2015. Web. 27 July 2015.

INDEX

About the Author

Alexandra (Alix) Morris is a health and science writer and global health specialist. Alix holds a master's in science writing from the Massachusetts Institute of Technology and a master's in health science from Johns Hopkins School of Public Health. Prior to science writing, Alix worked for pediatric telemedicine and HIV vaccine organizations and spent several years living and working in East Africa, where she conducted field studies on malaria research. Alix is currently a science writer at Earthwatch Institute, where she writes about climate change, ocean health, and conservation science. Alix lives in Boston, Massachusetts, with a dog that thinks she's a human and a cat that thinks she's a dog.